THE BIG JAGUARS
3½-LITRE TO 420G

Other Titles in the Crowood AutoClassics Series

AC Cobra	Brian Laban
Alfa Romeo: Spider, Alfasud and Alfetta GT	Davis G. Styles
Aston Martin: DB4, DB5 and DB6	Johnathan Wood
Aston Martin and Lagonda	David G. Styles
Austin Healey 100 and 3000 Series	Graham Robson
BMW M-Series	Alan Henry
Ferrari Dino	Anthony Curtis
Ford Capri	Mike Taylor
Jaguar E-Type	Jonathan Wood
Jaguar Mk 1 and 2	James Taylor
Jaguar XJ Series	Graham Robson
Jensen Interceptor	John Tipler
Lamborghini Countach	Peter Dron
Lotus and Caterham Seven	John Tipler
Lotus Elan	Mike Taylor
Lotus Esprit	Jeremy Walton
Mercedes SL Series	Brain Laban
MGB	Brain Laban
Morgan: The Cars and the Factory	John Tipler
Porsche 911	David Vivian
Porsche 924/928/944/968	David Vivian
Range Rover	James Taylor and Nick Dimbleby
Spoting Fords: Cortina to Cosworth	Mike Taylor
Sprites and Midgets	Anders Ditlev Clausager
Triumph TRs	Graham Robson
Triumph 2000 and 2.5PI	Graham Robson
TVR: The Complete Story	John Tipler

The Big Jaguars
3½ litre to 420G

Graham Robson

First published in 1995 by
The Crowood Press Ltd
Ramsbury, Marlborough
Wiltshire SN8 2HR

British Library Cataloguing in Publication Data

A catalogue record for this book is available from the British Library

ISBN 1 85223 922 0

Picture Credits
All photographs supplied by Micro Decet and the author

Printed and bound in Great Britain by The Bath Press

Contents

Acknowledgements

In effect it has taken me nearly forty years to write this book. Over those years, I readily acknowledge the debt I owe to everyone at Jaguar who has variously employed me, talked to me, listened to me, humoured me and helped me to assemble all the facts.

Although Sir William Lyons, 'Lofty' England and Bill Heynes were all impossibly important, remote figures during my years at Jaguar, from time to time they all greeted me courteously and civilly on business matters, and it was always easy to see how their various characters – and achievements – did so much to make Jaguar cars what they were. Claude Baily (engines), Tom Jones (chassis) and Bob Knight (development) were more readily accessible, as were other notable characters like Norman Dewis (chief test driver) and Bob 'Fangio' Berry (public relations).

Later, as a Coventry-based motoring writer for *Autocar*, I came to know 'Lofty' and Bob Berry much better. Having moved through the works in the same training 'tide' as Andrew Whyte in the 1950s, much later it was a pleasure to keep in contact with him as Jaguar's surviving PR man when British Leyland was going through its worst times – then and later, until his early and untimely death, he was the 'keeper of the flame' as far as Jaguar was concerned. This was also the period in which I came to know and admire those two engine-design geniuses, Walter Hassan and Harry Mundy. It was my privilege to help Walter Hassan write his autobiography in the 1970s, a task which Harry Mundy never allowed me to duplicate for him!

More recently, when the time came for me to write this and other Jaguar books, a mass of Jaguar PR staff, Jaguar enthusiasts and colleagues all helped: at Jaguar David Boole, Colin Cook, Joe Greenwell, Ann Harris and Val West all opened many doors, showed me filing cabinets to dig through, and generally made it easy to recreate my memories and impressions of Jaguar in the 1960s.

Specialists like Anders Clausager (BMIHT), Paul Skilleter (Jaguar authority), David Bishop (British Motor Heritage) and, of course, the late Andrew Whyte (all things Jaguar) have all provided assistance. John Parker, a good friend and Jaguar fanatic who from time to time has owned, loved and restored almost every model covered in this book, was a mine of information. And finally special thanks go to my good friend Mirco Decet, for locating and photographing the splendid Big Jaguars which feature in this book.

Jaguar Evolution

Although the original SS-Jaguar 3½-litre was announced in 1937 and series production of the 420G ended in 1970, there were many other important events which influenced their career:

Swallow Sidecars and SS Cars 1922–45

4 September 1901	William Lyons was born in Blackpool, Lancashire.
1922	Lyons and William Walmsley set up the Swallow Sidecar Company in Blackpool.
1927	First-ever SS-bodied car, an 'Austin Seven Swallow' produced.
1928	SS business moved, from Blackpool to Foleshill, Coventry.
1931	First-ever SS-badged car, the six-cylinder SSI, introduced. First deliveries followed in January 1932.
1934	A new company, SS Cars Ltd, was founded to replace Swallow.
January 1935	SS Cars was floated on the stock exchange, William Walmsley bowed out and William Lyons became the sole proprietor.
1935	First-ever SS-Jaguars introduced, with 1.6-litre and 2.6-litre engines. 3½-litre version (the first car covered in this book) was introduced in September 1937.
(1939–1945	Private car assembly interrupted by Second World War.)

Jaguar–the early days, 1945–52

March 1945	Company changes its name from SS Cars Ltd to Jaguar Cars Ltd.
July 1945	Post-war range announced, though deliveries did not begin until January 1946.
October 1948	Introduction of new Mk V model, with independent front suspension, but retaining old-style pushrod ohv six cylinder engine. Preview of XK120 sports car, powered by Jaguar's brand-new six-cylinder twin ohc XK engine. XK120 deliveries began in 1949.
October 1950	Launch of XK-engined Mk VII saloon model.

| June 1951 | Final deliveries of Mk V models and final use of pushrod ohv engines. Henceforth, all attention was concentrated on XK-engined cars. |
| 1951–52 | Gradual move of all Jaguar facilities from Foleshill to the Browns Lane, Allesley, factory. The move was complete in November 1952. |

Jaguar at Browns Lane, 1952–6

October 1954	Mk VIIM replaced the original Mk VII.
October 1956	Mk VIII supplemented the Mk VIIM, though Mk VIIM deliveries continued until July 1957.
October 1958	Mk IX supplemented the Mk VIII, though Mark VIII deliveries continued until December 1959.
May 1960	Jaguar absorbed the Daimler company. New 'Daimler' models developed by Jaguar followed from 1962.
March 1961	Introduction of new E-Type sports car, which featured the use of independent rear suspension, of a type to be shared with future Jaguar saloons.
September 1961	Last deliveries of separate-chassis Mk IX.

The Biggest Jaguars of all, 1961–92

October 1961	Introduction of Mk X saloon, the largest-ever Jaguar, with unit-construction bodyshell, 3.8-litre engine and all-independent suspension.
October 1964	Mk X (4.2-litre) replaced Mk X (3.8-litre), the first of these cars to have an all-synchromesh gearbox.
Summer 1966	Jaguar merged with BMC, to become part of British Motor Holdings. No immediate effect on Jaguar company policy.
October 1966	420G, a slightly re-worked version, took over from the 4.2 litre Mk X.
January 1968	Foundation of British Leyland, when BMH merged with Leyland Motors. No immediate effect on Jaguar policy.
June 1968	Launch of new Daimler limousine, a Jaguar design using a stretched (by 21in /533mm) Mk X platform and running gear, but a Vanden Plas completed bodyshell.
October 1968	Introduction of XJ6 model, eventually to take over from all older-model Jaguars.
June 1970	Final deliveries of 420G models.
8 February 1985	Death of Sir William Lyons.
1992	Final deliveries of Daimler limousine, this bringing to an end the long-running saga of the 420G-based model.

Introduction

There is a very personal element to this account, and it all revolves around Joe Barker. Joe who? you might ask. This book, you see, is not a 'cuttings job', but was inspired by my years at Jaguar in the late 1950s and early 1960s when the Mk VII family was at its height, the Mk 2 models were being developed and the Mk X ('Zenith', to me) was being styled.

Joe Barker was Jaguar's Training Manager, the man who took me on, fresh from university, in August 1957. It is only now, looking back, that I admire so much his decision to give me a chance, and how grateful I still am. After all, there I was, an engineering graduate, looking to design cars, cocky as you like and quite convinced that Jaguar would rush to make me an offer when I approached them. Which was all well and good, except that at that time Jaguar's design department was small and there simply was no graduate scheme. A group of bright young apprentices were already working their way through the factory in the 1950s – among them Andrew Whyte (later the respected and now much-missed Jaguar historian), Trevor Crisp (who became Jaguar's chief engine designer), David Fielden (later Quality Director) and Dick Soans (who went on to run the family Ford franchise in Leamington Spa) – but a different scheme had to be worked out before I arrived.

A lot of the detail in this book came my way in the years surrounding my stay in various departments and in my work in the famous Jaguar design offices. Scars on my hands still remind me of time spent on the XK crankshaft machining line, and on help-ing to make checking jigs for XK150 soft tops. Every time I look back at period pictures I remember why the original E-Type exhaust system had to look so obvious from the rear, why there was a carefully crafted bend in the dipstick of certain XK engine types, why the Mk X's rear suspension radius arms look the way they do, and how the Mk IX's automatic gearbox shift lever was actually connected to the Borg Warner box itself. They all took shape on my drawing board.

In the 1950s and 1960s, like almost all young motoring enthusiasts, I backed Jaguar in all its sporting exploits. Most of all I was always particularly impressed by the way the 'works' Mk VIIs won Saloon Car races at Silverstone. But there was more. Once I joined Jaguar, I became one of those lucky people who spend hours driving, or being a passenger in, the new Jaguars of the day. Yes, there were times when we really did drive newly minted Mk VIIIs around factory roads using component boxes to sit on instead of seats and we really did get a chance to sample XK150s before they went off to their customers. Oh, and by the way, that story about a new XK150 being speared by a forklift truck as it sped around a factory corner is absolutely true – it was being driven by an apprentice, but luckily not by me.

Working on, under, around and inside the big Jaguar saloons was always a pleasure and to me, as a learner, it was also an education. Stripping out or assembling a new model taught all of us how and where Jaguar engineering was so supreme, where the heritage came from and where money had been so sensibly saved. When we were working in 'Experimental' it also taught us not to fool around, for we never knew when the impressive blue-suited figure of Sir William Lyons would bustle into sight, often with Bill Heynes or Bob Knight in close attendance.

All of us soon learned how Jaguar extracted value for all its efforts, how new ideas quickly came to fruition, and how the Jaguar philosophy permeated through the workforce. Once I was installed on a drawing board at Browns Lane, I soon found out what was likely to appeal to Bill Heynes and his lieutenants – and what did not.

Over in one corner that legendary aerodynamicist, Malcolm Sayer, sat immersed in mountains of calculations, creating graceful lines on paper, and occasionally studied a small-scale wooden wind-tunnel model which had been produced to test his theories. Much of his time was spent on sports-car design, but he still found time to look at more mundane shapes and to cast an eye at saloon car shapes Sir William proposed: the Mk X was one of them. For all of us, it was all very well slaving away on a new layout for days (there were no CAD screens, computers or electronic calculators in those days, everything had to be done with tables of logarithms, slide rules, and hard pencils on waxy paper), but if design chiefs did not like what they saw this effort could be instantly scarred with a few sketchy sweeps of a softer pencil.

Although this was the time when the compact Mk 1 and Mk 2 saloons came to dominate the scene at Browns Lane, it was still a period when the big Jaguars were important members of the Jaguar range. None of us ever forgot that the Mk VII had been the world's first series-production saloon car to have a twin-cam engine, that its successors were still there, selling steadily, and being exported in large quantities.

When the 'Zenith' (Mk X), complete with all-independent suspension, eventually came along, every member of the design team realized what a technological leap it actually was. Until the chassis designers saw Sir William's agreed style they had very little idea of the new car they were committing to multi-million pound tooling, but once the first cars took to the road everyone felt better about it all.

This book, therefore, is a celebration of all the largest post-war saloons. It covers more than twenty-five eventful years at Jaguar and what I still affectionately call the 'Big Jaguars'. Over the years they have tended to be outshone by the more glamorous Mk 2s and XJ6s, and certainly overshadowed by Jaguar's amazing sports cars. Yet they were, and still are, important members of the Jaguar family.

This, I hope, is the complete story of those fine machines.

1 Ancestors: SS, Standard and SS-Jaguar

It takes some believing, but it is true – the sleekly styled, twin-cam-engined Jaguar Mk VIIs and Mk Xs of the 1950s and 1960s were direct descendants of a series of spidery sidecars, for use with motorcycles, which were built in Blackpool in the 1920s. Even more remarkable is the fact that Jaguar, the definitive marque founded in 1945, is the most recent British marque to become and remain a major player on the world's motoring stage. Other makes of car, such as Lotus, have flared up but stayed small, while many other long-established names have died.

There is something unique, surely, about a company which always offered so much, and was a pioneer, where other longer-established companies were content to coast. Jaguar and its predecessors always sold cars at remarkably low prices. Its cars were invariably faster and more strikingly styled than its rivals. Jaguar was the first to offer a twin-ohc engine in series production, the first to use disc brakes in a racing car, and the first to race cars with bodies using mathematically, rather than artistically, derived shapes.

None of this, of course, could have happened without Sir William Lyons, who *was* Jaguar from the beginning, until his retirement in 1972, and this book must start with a summary of how he built up his business.

MODEST BEGINNINGS

Although the name 'Jaguar' first appeared

Early Swallow sidecars of the 1920s looked like this, with rakish lines quite unlike those offered by rival manufacturers. But times change. Swallow eventually evoved into Jaguar, while the company which built the motorcyle – Rover – became one of Britain's largest car-makers.

11

Sir William Lyons (1901–85)

Along with William Walmsley, Blackpool-born William Lyons founded the Swallow sidecar building business, then followed up with SS Cars, before becoming sole proprietor in 1935. He invented the Jaguar marque name in 1935, saw his company become world-famous after the Second World War and was 'Mr Jaguar' until the day he retired in 1972.

During his working life William Lyons, who had a faultless eye for a line despite his lack of formal training, shaped every Jaguar production car except the E-Type (which was a direct evolution of the D-Type and therefore Malcolm Sayers' responsibility). This ensured that there was always a recognizable connection between one Jaguar and the next, and it meant that 'the Jaguar look' was always instantly recognizable all over the world. Today's designers can still see identifiable 'cues' linking the 3½-litre of the 1930s with the Mk VII of the 1950s, and with the Mk X of the 1960s. He even insisted that the XK engine should look right as well as being very powerful.

Sir William (he was knighted in 1956) was always respected by his workforce, though never loved, as he was reputedly a hard taskmaster. He liked to keep a formal atmosphere in his business, calling even his closest colleagues by their surnames and keeping them personally at arm's length. Some of this reserve was almost certainly caused by the death of his only son, and heir, and his need to make sure that he showed no personal or business favours to anyone.

Not only was Sir William Lyons an accomplished and successful stylist, he was also an astute businessman and a talented chooser of staff. It was no accident that Jaguar Cars grew and prospered while rival companies (Daimler and Armstrong-Siddeley being perfect examples) struggled to survive.

To underpin Jaguar's future after he had gone, he agreed to merge with BMC in 1966, this then leading his company to become a part of British Leyland in 1968. Until the day he retired, however, Sir William Lyons protected the technical and styling independence of his cars – the merger with Daimler, for instance, leading to Jaguar ideas being incorporated into Daimler cars, but not the other way around.

After retiring, he continued to visit the factory which he had built up, though he was known to be disappointed by the fallow years which followed British Leyland's traumas. However, before he died, at 84 years old, he was once again content to see Jaguar privatized and prosperous.

on motor cars in 1935, the story really began in 1922, when the young William Lyons joined forces with William Walmsley, to start building sidecars for motorcycles in a factory in Blackpool. Then, as for the next fifty years, it was Lyons who shaped the products. Then, as in the future, it was always Lyons who had a vision of the future – as he wanted it to be.

This story, therefore, must chart the rapid growth of a concern which first built Swallow sidecars, then Swallow-bodied cars, then SS cars, and followed up by launching the SS-Jaguar – all within thirteen incident-packed years.

Although Blackpool-born William Lyons

is always seen as the accomplished stylist-businessman, there was no such heritage in his family background. When he left school, unqualified, at seventeen years of age, he first thought of getting an apprenticeship at Vickers (the giant shipbuilding Company at Barrow-in-Furness), then took up an apprenticeship at Crossley Motors Ltd, who were based in Manchester.

It was his interest in motorcycles which brought him into contact with sidecars, and it was only after forging a partnership with William Walmsley (to set up the Swallow Sidecar Company) that he began to influence the shape of products. Then, as for years to follow, Swallow's products were

William Lyons in early life in Blackpool, when his principal interest was with motorcycles and the shaping of sidecars to sell with them. That bike, incidentally, is a vee-twin Harley Davidson from the USA, stripped and ready for use in motorcycle sport.

This picture linked sixty years of engineering, Swallow with Jaguar, when taken after the late-1980s launch of the 'XJ40' type saloon. The Austin Seven Swallow was one of the very first car styles by William Lyons – actually in Blackpool – and was therefore a true ancestor of all the other cars described in this book.

Swallow offered special open and closed bodies on the ubiquitous Austin chassis, this being the rounded and 'oh-so-small' four-seater saloon of the late 1920s.

always considered more shapely than those of their rivals.

After Swallow had repaired and rebodied several cars in the mid-1920s, the next move was to start building special bodies for new car chassis. With the company name changed to the Swallow Sidecar and Coach Building Company, the company put the first of these – the Austin Seven Swallow – on sale in 1927. For the Austin Seven, which normally had a craggy style with a slab-vertical radiator, a new and more curvaceous style was evolved. Complete with a rounded nose, a vee-screen, and a curvaceous, rather 'sexy', rump, the aluminium-bodied Austin Seven made all other small cars looked ordinary.

That was precisely what William Lyons had in mind – he wanted to make every other car look ordinary, wanted to set the trends, and was already determined to move up to bigger, better and more profitable ventures. Even though production was disrupted for a time in 1928, when the business was moved from Blackpool to Foleshill, Coventry, in the Whitmore Park estate, progress was astonishingly rapid. The original Austin Seven Swallow was introduced in May 1927, the Morris-Cowley-Swallow followed in the same year, a Fiat-Swallow and a Swift-Swallow in 1929, then a Wolseley Hornet-Swallow from 1931. The most significant model of them all, however, the Standard-Swallow, arrived in 1930.

FORGING THE STANDARD CONNECTION

Although the Swallow styling pedigree was well-established by 1931, and thousands of special bodies were being produced every year, William Lyons and his backers were not satisfied. According to legendary Jaguar historian, the late Andrew Whyte:

Henly, Hough and Lyons ... were seeing that Swallow's style would be as short-lived as that of its rivals if a special chassis could not be produced at a reasonable cost, to accommodate the long low look they wanted to sell. The characteristic Swallow saloon had reached its ultimate expression, having been 'stretched' from Austin Seven out to Standard Sixteen dimensions.

Lyons, in fact, was becoming frustrated by having to adapt his thoughts on body design to existing chassis from other manufacturers, which often did not come up to his standards of performance, or of dimensions. Ideally he would have liked to be able to use longer and lower frames, so that his Swallow styles could themselves be leaner and more sporting.

Accordingly, Lyons and Walmsley resolved to take the big step of introducing a car of their manufacture – or, rather, a car of their own assembly. This was the genesis of the SS, and the reason that I make this point so carefully is that for the first few years in the 1930s the only section of an SS car actually to be manufactured at Foleshill was the bodyshell.

Walmsley, the businessman rather than the visionary, left the choice of design to Lyons, who instinctively favoured the sports saloons and drophead coupés for which his company would become famous in the future. Choosing to produce a gracious, long and low car, rather than something small and chubby like the original Standard Swallows, he then cast around for a suitable chassis. Enter the Standard Motor Company Ltd and its energetic and capable, not to say truly likeable, general manager, Captain John Black. This one-time Tank Corps officer and earlier trainee patents specialist, had joined Hillman in 1919, where he wooed and won one of William Hillman's six daughters. Following the arrival of the Rootes family on the scene at Hillman in 1928, John Black moved out, becoming Standard's general manager at a critical period in its history.

Black, the talented organizer and a manager with single-minded determination to get his own way, then set about modernizing and expanding Standard. Within a year he became a director and before long Standard's founder R.W. Maudslay saw him as the company's eventual boss. The Standard Motor Company Ltd, with an ever-expanding business at Canley, on the western edge of Coventry (about four miles away from the Whitmore Park estate), was clearly ambitious and was amply large enough to supply all SS's needs.

It was under Black, with Ted Grinham (also ex-Humber) as his chief engineer, that a new side-valve four/six-cylinder family of engines was developed, along with chassis which to William Lyons seemed to be more suitable than any others on which he had worked. The 1931 range included the 2,054cc Ensign and the 2,522cc Envoy models, both with the notably smooth six-cylinder engines, which had seven-main-bearing crankshafts, allied to four-speed gearboxes. Wheelbases were 109in (2,769mm) and 118in (2,997mm).

Clearly William Lyons liked what he saw, for during 1931 he introduced the Standard Ensign-Swallow (which sold for £275), but this was only a prelude to what was to come. In a fascinating commercial arrangement, Lyons had already asked Rubery Owen, chassis design specialists, to produce a special new chassis frame for Swallow's use, which would then be supplied to Standard for them to complete, and to deliver to Swallow as a complete rolling chassis.

The new frame had a 112in (2,845mm) wheelbase – the dimension fell half-way between those of the large Standards – with an entirely different profile when viewed from the side. However, except for the use of flatter half-elliptic leaf springs, the running gear was all shared with Standards

(renamed) 'Sixteen' and 'Twenty' hp models for 1932.

SS – A NEW MARQUE IS BORN

As *The Autocar* wrote in July 1931:

> 'S.S.' is the new symbol adopted for a new car which will be put on the market in due course by the Swallow Coachbuilding Co .... The car is a marvellously low-built two-seater coupé of most modern line .... The mechanism of the car has been developed from the 1932 type Standard Sixteen chassis ....

S.S. or SS? Should we care about the grammar, and the punctuation marks, or doesn't it matter? 'S.S.' was used in the original descriptions, but all the production cars were called 'SS', so let's leave it at that.

In any case, what did it all mean? Over the years many options were explored, but no one, not even William Lyons, ever made a decision. S.S. had previously featured on George Brough's famous motorcycles, but as Sir William once recalled: 'There was much speculation as to whether S.S. stood for Standard Swallow, or Swallow Special – it was never resolved'.

The very first SS-badged cars – the six-cylinder SSI (which cost £310) and the much smaller Standard Nine-chassis'd SSII (£210) – were previewed at the Olympia Motor Show in October 1931, deliveries began in January 1932 and no fewer than 776 were delivered in that year.

Then, as later, the styling of an SS was more remarkable than the performance, for there is little doubt that the Standard engines were worthy rather than powerful, the chassis durable rather than sporting. Year on year, though, the style of the cars evolved, shapes getting progressively longer, wider, sleeker, and with more flowing lines,

This was the very first 'teaser' advert for the new six-cylinder SS marque, as it appeared in The Autocar *on October 1931. In the flesh, the SSI's cabin was considerably deeper than as drawn in the advert – no fully-grown driver, surely, could have been comfortable inside the sketched machine!*

particularly with respect to the wings and the cabin shapes.

STYLING OF THE SS

When it came to shaping his cars, William Lyons always knew what he wanted, but often took a long time to reach that point. When a new car was being shaped, he would try mock-up after mock-up, ruthlessly scrapping styles that he did not like and often trying ideas 'in the round' just to see what they looked like. What's more, a style or detail which he liked one day might no longer be good enough for him the morning after. In this, as in so many other aspects of his business life, he was decisive. In those days, if not in the 1950s and 1960s, his language could be salty, especially if he could not get his ideas across.

The interpreter of his dreams was Fred Gardner, who nominally ran the saw mill for many years, but eventually ended up copying down Lyons' ideas on car styling. Fred and his craftsmen would build the wooden mock-ups of proposed new shapes, then modify them and further modify them to his instructions until he was finally satisfied. It was all done by discussion, not from the interpretation of drawings, for Lyons rarely sought to sketch, always preferring to work 'in the round', and always full-size rather than in a smaller scale.

Owing to the fact that the style of the original SSI was completed in his absence, when Lyons was away from the factory, laid low for weeks by an appendix operation, it must rank as something of an aberration. Even so, it spelt out the basic theme of SS and SS-Jaguar cars to come for some time, with a long, low look, a lengthy bonnet and a rather restricted cabin. Even so, it was the revised model of September 1932 which really set the trends. With a longer wheelbase (close to the magic 120in (3,048mm)

which would be used by every large Jaguar of the next three decades), and with a substantially revised chassis, the latest cars had long, flowing wing lines, huge headlamps set high at each side of the radiator, a low roof line and a small oblong-shaped rear window with rounded-off corners. Sidelamps were atop the front wings, horns with chrome-plated grilles were carried below the headlamps on the front bumper, while the radiator grille was vertically-striped, with a pronounced vee-profile.

If this was the master's signature, he changed it only gradually in the next few years. By 1935, when even the largest SS models still only had two-door coachwork, the grille seemed to be lying back a little more, the screen seemed to be slightly lower and certain styling 'cues' around the cabin had settled down.

There was, however, one lasting problem, which would hang around the cars for some years to come. Right from the start the company had acquired a rather 'flash' reputation, though there was no good reason for this. For the hide-bound middle classes of Britain, it caused a problem. Helped along by a whispering campaign from rivals, there were suggestions that it still wasn't the right sort of car to be seen in. 'Well, yes, they are very pretty, but, old boy, somehow they're not a gentleman's car, are they...?'

Older-established companies, particularly those likely to suffer from SS's rapid expansion, were anxious to play up their own traditions, and to denigrate the achievements of the upstarts. There were suggestions that an SS was all style and no performance (that, at least, was partly true at first), that the low selling price of an SS had only been achieved by skimping on quality (which was nonsense) and that it was courting social death to buy one.

Later, when the SS-Jaguars came along, with real performance and magnificent styling, the criticism, quite unfounded, got

By the end of 1933 several different types of body style had been launched for the SSI. This was the 1934-model saloon, which in its most powerful form had a 68bhp 2.7-litre side-valve six-cylinder engine. It rode on a 119in (3,023mm) wheelbase – only 1in (25mm) shorter than the 'classic' dimension used by every Big Jaguar in the 1950s and 1960s.

more pointed. SS-Jaguar adopted the telegraphic address of 'Bentley's Second', which may not have been wise, because the cars were soon called 'Jews' Bentleys'. From the end of 1935, when the SS-Jaguar came on the scene, the criticism became positively hysterical. And if you had been a director or a dealer of Triumph, of Riley or of Rover cars then you could have been justified in joining in....

MOVING TOWARDS INDEPENDENCE

In 1935 the entire business stepped up another gear. SS Cars Ltd, a new subsidiary company set up in 1933, offered its shares on the stock exchange, stating that it was taking over all the operations of Swallow Coachbuilding. Swallow's original partners had already split up a few weeks earlier, for

William Walmsley sold up, walked away from the business and left William Lyons as the chairman and sole managing director of his rapidly expanding company.

At flotation time, it was revealed that SS businesses had made £72,000 since the SSI had gone on sale. The issue of new shares raised around £180,000, which Lyons needed to finance the range of new cars that he was already planning. These would not only replace the SSIs and SSIIs, but would move SS Cars Ltd into a new league. Although Lyons could still not afford to see his company design and build its own engines, for 1936 and beyond he wanted to build better, more powerful and faster cars which would be unique in most other respects. He wanted to offer a new range of 90mph (145km/h) machines with different engines, different chassis – and a new model name. From SS, not only would these cars be the first to have four passenger doors, but the first to have overhead-valve engines.

Amazingly, in their first three years, SS cars had prospered and developed without an engineering department of any sort. All the mechanical engineering on the car had been carried out by Standard (at Canley) or by Rubery Owen (in Darlaston). Body engineering, like styling, had been done 'in the round', there being no draughtsmen and no drawings, only jigs and craftsmen to duplicate the original shapes. For 1935 and beyond, Lyons wanted to begin breaking free of Standard. He was happy to carry on buying running gear from them at first, but wanted to reduce his reliance gradually in the future. Accordingly, not only did his 'master plan' require new engines and a new style, but it also needed an engineering department to design the chassis and all the other components.

While work began in Fred Gardner's shop on a new body style – not unusual since something different was always being developed in the styling field – William Lyons began to wrestle with the problem of finding more powerful engines and new chassis designs. Then, as later, it was going to take longer to develop new engines, so he concentrated on this problem first. Happy with his business relationships with Standard (though always having to be careful in his personal dealings with Black), he was reluctant to look elsewhere, even though the side-valve 'sixes' were not very lusty. In any case, more powerful engines of the appropriate size were almost all made by his rivals and were therefore not available. This, therefore, presented a problem.

These were the days in which a few motoring journalists – *The Autocar's* S.C.H. 'Sammy' Davis, *The Motor's* Laurence Pomeroy, and Fleet Street's Tommy Wisdom among them – were all accomplished 'fixers', who seemed to know what was brewing, who wanted help, and where the spare expertise could be found. In this case it was Tommy Wisdom who introduced Harry Weslake to William Lyons.

In 1934 Weslake, an engineering consultant and self-taught expert in enhancing the power output of engines by improving their airflow, had recently quarrelled with MG's Cecil Kimber and was looking for any obvious way to get back at him. Tommy Wisdom heard of this and, realizing that Standard could not help William Lyons to improve on the 70bhp of their 2.7-litre side-valve engine, arranged a meeting.

Weslake was a forceful, not to say cocky, character while William Lyons was proudly independent but more formal. When the two met at Foleshill, therefore, a certain amount of friction had to be overcome. Many years later, Weslake claimed that he greeted Lyons with: 'Your car reminds me of an over-dressed woman with no brains – there's nothing under the bonnet!' Lyons, though taken aback by this, nevertheless supposed that Weslake knew what should be done, whereupon the Exeter-born engineer stated that he needed an overhead-valve engine. The outcome of this was that SS gave Weslake a consultancy contract to produce an overhead-valve conversion of the six-cylinder Standard engine (Black was not told about this at first!), his target being to produce at least 95bhp.

Having designed a very simple new cast-iron head, with overhead valves, lozenge-shaped combustion chambers, and with twin SU carburettors bolted to an inlet manifold/gallery which was cast into the head itself, Weslake astonished everyone (maybe even himself) by recording 103bhp. The torque curve looked good, the Standard-based bottom end was clearly solid enough and conversion costs looked reasonable, so William Lyons was well pleased. From that day forward, Harry Weslake became a trusted advisor to the company. Lyons then used

his fabled diplomatic skills to advise John Black of his plans, to persuade him to manufacture special overhead-valve versions of the six-cylinder head and to invest in the machining plant needed to make the heads in quantity. (After the event, I am told, John Black could still not quite believe that he had agreed to this ....)

By the spring of 1935, Lyons was determined to preview his new range at the Olympia Motor Show, but he still didn't have an engineering department or a chief designer to produce a chassis for him. Where could he find the right man? Once again the Coventry 'motor-industry-mafia' swung into operation. Standard's chief engineer was Ted Grinham, who had previously worked at Humber Ltd on the other side of the city, where he knew that a bright young man called William Heynes had replaced him as

William Heynes (1903–89)

Before Bill Heynes started work for William Lyons in 1935, the company really had no engineering department. With plans for the original SS-Jaguars already being made, Lyons hired him to change all that. By the 1950s Jaguar's technical resources had mushroomed, the company's twin-cam XK engine was famous and its racing reputation was already established.

William Munger Heynes was born in Leamington Spa, near Coventry, attended Warwick school, where the masters suggested that he should train to become a surgeon. Instead he joined Humber Ltd as an apprentice, ran the technical department there from 1930, remaining until April 1935 when he joined SS Cars Ltd in Foleshill.

His speciality at this time was chassis and suspension design, which perfectly balanced William Lyons's love of body styling and engineering. As Chief Engineer of SS, and with only one draughtsman to assist him, his first job was to finalize the new SS-Jaguar models, after which he masterminded the design of the overhead-valve engines which served SS-Jaguar, and later Jaguar, until the end of the 1940s.

After joining the Board of Directors in 1946 and before retiring from Jaguar in 1969, he became the company's Engineering Director, then Vice Chairman (Engineering). Although Sir William Lyons never admitted as much, Heynes was his indispensable right-hand-man for many successful years. It was under the control of Heynes that the classic XK engine, the XK120 sports car, the Mk V, Mk VII and Mk X saloons, the compact Mk 1 and Mk 2 saloons, the famous C-Type, D-Type and E-Type models and the XJ6 were all developed. The now-legendary V12 engine, too, was well on its way to launch before he retired at the age of 66.

Heynes was always a dapper little man, who inspired rather than drew the cars for which he was responsible. He was addicted to what his drawing-office staff used to call 'the 4B pencil redesign job', and ran his engineering departments like a personal fiefdom. Subordinates like Claude Baily, Walter Hassan and Bob Knight were all experts in their own way, but it was Heynes, who could be stubborn as well as dismissive, who always got his way in the end.

head of the Stress Office.

On the grapevine, Grinham already knew that Heynes, a resourceful and forward-looking 32-year-old engineer, was unhappy working under the stifling yoke of Humber's chief engineer, Bernard Winter. Ever-obedient to the penny-pinching Rootes family's demands, Winter was running something of a cheap-and-cheerful philistine's operation (current Hillman and Humber designs were uninspired, to say the least), and Heynes was thought to be ready to leave.

Discreet enquiries were made, Heynes was interviewed, Lyons was eventually satisfied, and in April 1935 a two-man engineering department swung into action; his only assistant was draughtsman Percy Smith. It may also have needed all the help that Rubery Owen could give, but the miracle was achieved and a new chassis was ready for production in September, only five months later.

In the meantime, Lyons had spent much time agonizing over new names to be given to his new range of cars. This was imperative because he was moving the marque up-market, with more performance, and because somehow he wanted to fight free of the 'cad's car' image which had grown up around SS. As Andrew Whyte wrote in his company history:

> Now that SS Cars was moving forward at such a pace, there was a growing feeling that the next new product should have a name of its own. The word 'Standard' kept cropping up – with and without the 'Swallow' bit. If 'SS' did not stand for anything in particular, the public were not getting much chance to believe it....
>
> Earlier in 1935, Lyons thought that he had secured the assets of the bankrupt Sunbeam concern, but he was eventually out-manoeuvred by the Rootes Group. The 'Sunbeam' name would have been ideal to apply to the new cars, but this was no

longer possible. At short notice, therefore, he was forced to start again. Having taken advice from his advertising agency and his publicity chief Bill Rankin, a short-list of animal, fish and bird names was assembled. Some names had already been adopted as trademarks by other car companies, but in the end 'Jaguar' was chosen. Armstrong-Siddeley, which made Jaguar aero-engines, readily gave their permission. Just in time, the new name of SS-Jaguar was chosen, suitable badges were designed and the product could finally be launched.

THE SS-JAGUAR

After a year of frantic behind-the-scenes activity, the SS-Jaguar was finally revealed in October 1935. The even bigger miracle was that the Foleshill factory had been re-equipped, most of the ageing SSI and SSII body tooling had been cast aside and the new car was ready for deliveries to begin.

During 1935 the two-man engineering team expanded slightly, with engine-man Laurie Hathaway arriving from Hotchkiss (which became Morris Engines), and with body-engineer Bill Thornton arriving from Triumph (which was next door to SS in Foleshill).

For 1936 there were to be two closely related SS-Jaguar saloons. One of them was the newly developed 2.7-litre six-cylinder car, most confusingly called a 2½-litre. The other was a shorter-wheelbase derivative with the existing Standard side-valve four-cylinder engine of 1,608cc as used in the current SSII models – this being known as the '1½-litre'.

Owing to the short time available to them, Heynes's team could not design an all-new chassis frame for these new cars, instead having to modify the existing 1935 model SSI variety. The existing wheelbase (at 119in (3,023mm), it was just 1in (25mm)

Foleshill Factory (1928–52)

The first SS-Jaguars, all the Mk Vs and the first Mk VIIs were all produced in the Foleshill factory, in Swallow Road, which Jaguar had occupied since 1928. This was in the ex-First World War Whitmore Park estate to the north of the city centre. By the time the Mk VII came on the scene, the Foleshill plant was bursting at the seams.

As originally used by Swallow, the factory, erected some years earlier as shell-filling units for the First World War effort, used two of the four separate blocks connected by very scruffy (sometimes muddy) estate roads. Two of the other blocks had actually been disused for ten years when Swallow arrived.

Leasing the original block, then buying the others in 1933, SS, SS-Jaguar and then Jaguar Cars soon filled them. The estate road soon became 'Swallow Road' and was made up, a new office block was erected, adjoining factories were taken over by one of SS-Jaguar's rivals, Triumph, while SS Cars eventually took over Motor Panels Ltd, whose premises were also in the same industrial estate.

Then came the Second World War, during which SS Cars Ltd built a new factory block (much larger than their existing premises) next to their own premises, which was intended for the assembly of aircraft structures. It was in watching over this complex, to guard against fire bombing, that the Heynes/Baily/Hassan team started designing the XK engine.

With hostilities coming to an end, Jaguar Cars was born, the Motor Panels business was sold off, and car assembly eventually began in the modern factory block. A factory fire in 1947 did little to hold back the business, which was soon building more than 100 cars a week. By 1950, though, more scope for expansion was needed, even though the original 40,000sq ft building of 1928 had already grown to 600,000sq ft.

New buildings on adjacent virgin land were envisaged, but planning permission was refused. As a result, William Lyons began negotiating to acquire the Browns Lane factory instead. The move out of Foleshill began in 1951 and was completed by the autumn of 1952. Jaguar then sold off the premises to other Midlands-based concerns, including Dunlop, and concentrated on building up its operations at Browns Lane.

---

shorter than the 'standard' 120in (3,048mm) dimension that would come to be so well known in future decades) was retained for the 2½-litre, as were the same basic side members and the cruciform member. The frame was widened and there were new boxed-sectioned areas of the main side members, and the rear suspension leaf springs had been repositioned inside the line of the side members, which still passed under the line of the back axle.

The same type of front axle beam, rear spiral-bevel axle and leaf-spring suspension layouts were carried forward, though innovations included the use of Burman worm-and-nut steering gear and Girling mechanical brakes. Amazingly, at the rear the Luvax hydraulic lever-arm suspension dampers were mounted on the axle, rather than on the chassis frame, which can have done nothing for the sprung/unsprung weight ratio.

Mechanically, the 2½-litre model looked fabulous, for the new Weslake-inspired 2,663cc overhead-valve engine developed 102bhp, and since the engine had a polished aluminium cover for the valve gear, every one of them seemed to be on show. Behind the engine there was a Flying Standard type of four-speed gearbox with synchromesh on second, third and top gears – though with a specially developed remote-control gear change–and the existing type of spiral bevel differential was used. Although SS claimed a top speed of 'up to 90mph' (145km/h), independent tests showed a true maximum of 86mph (138km/h), but even this lower figure was still superior to that of rival models.

The body style of the new car, developed painstakingly from a wooden mock-up in the previous twelve months, was the first-ever four-door saloon to be put on sale by SS. A comparison with the most recent SSI two-door saloons showed evolution, rather than revolution in the shaping of the car.

Using the same wheelbase, almost the same wheel tracks and the same 5.5 × 18in tyres on centre-lock wire-spoke wheels, the new SS-Jaguar clearly had a larger, wider

and more capacious cabin, but in many ways the styling cues were the same. The 'signature', certainly, was the same.

The cabin was relatively further forward than before, the bonnet being correspondingly shorter. At the rear there was a more shapely, less angular, tail, complete with let-down boot lid: this new style was made possible by mounting the spare wheel under a cover tucked in to the near-side sweep of the front wing panel. Interestingly, in the original SS-Jaguar adverts of September 1935,

Mrs Lyons (later to become Lady Lyons) used this splendidly detailed black 2½-litre SS-Jaguar saloon in the late 1930s. Many of that car's styling 'cues' would be carried over for later cars, even up to and including the Mk V model of 1948–51. In one respect, though, we might suggest that these cars were less than safe – both front and rear doors hinged at the rear, which was excellent for entry and exit, but potentially dangerous if opened (and caught by the wind) while the car was still moving forward. A 1986-model Jaguar Sovereign V12 can be seen in the background.

that spare was shown mounted on the off side.

Another change made at a late stage was to the hanging of the doors. Strangely, whereas all SS-Jaguar 1½-litre/2½-litre production cars had front and rear doors hinged at the rear (this gave the easiest and most dignified access to the seats, even though in later years the layout was generally rejected on safety grounds), on the prototype shown to SS dealers in September the rear doors were hinged at the front, on the centre pillar.

More of the car's underpinnings were covered up than before, at the front this being done by bringing the shapely curve of the front wing almost down to bumper level and by filling in the valances behind the front wheels themselves. The radiator grille, while clearly developed from that of the SSI, was subtly squatter than before and took up a stance familiar to owners of Mk Vs too.

Inside the car, the trim and furnishings were a further evolution from the SSI, complete with characteristic 'sunrise-effect' pleats on the door trim panels and seats. Naturally there was a good deal of walnut veneer capping – on the doors and the facia – but on this model the centre arm-rest on the rear seat could be folded up, for this was not only a genuine four-seater car, but had flat cushioning across the back seat.

Independent road tests, with detailed diagrams, showed that the rear seat was 50in (127cm) wide and although this was considered good for its day, post-war style makes it seem rather constricted today. Rear seat legroom was distinctly restricted, but this would be improved after the first year. The boot too, by modern standards, looks tiny – and we must also remember that there was no heating and ventilation system, not even as an optional extra! SS had nothing to be ashamed of here, for this was normal for every British car-maker of the day.

There was the full array of instruments which sporting drivers expected in a 1930s

model, along with a springy four-spoke steering wheel; the telescopic column was a nice touch, as was the short-throw gearchange and the vertical handbrake positioned alongside the tunnel.

Alongside the new 102bhp six-cylinder car, SS also introduced the 1½-litre model, which had only a 108in (2,743mm) wheelbase (the shortening being concentrated in the engine bay area), narrower wheeltracks and smaller brakes. Because the engine was only a 52bhp 1.6-litre side-valve model, performance was way down on the 2½-litre, and although it was still excellent value for money (and sold well accordingly), it was really rather a sluggish machine which struggled even to reach 70mph (110km/h).

To complete the range, there was also the 2½-litre Sports Tourer, which was really a mixture of old-type SSI Tourer body running on the new chassis, complete with new engine, and the fierce, short-chassis, two-seater SS100 sports car.

SS-JAGUAR ON SALE

Jaguar previewed the new cars in September 1935 at a famous dinner held in London at which dealers, asked to suggest the selling price of the new 2½-litre, overestimated by a large margin. When Lyons revealed an initial selling price of £385 – and £285 for the 1½-litre – there was astonishment, followed by thunderous applause. As he later wrote:

With two scrutinizers from the gathering as supervisors, a comptometer operator calculated the average of all the prices [estimates] handed in. This came to £632, so when I announced that the actual price was £385, it created quite a lot of excitement and, indeed, added much enthusiasm for the car.

The SS100 sports car of the late 1930s was one of the 'sexiest' open cars ever designed, and though it sold only in limited numbers, did a great deal for SS-Jaguar's image. The engine, gearbox and axle were all shared with SS-Jaguar saloons of the day, most of this drive line also featuring in the Mk IV models which followed. Caught outside the front door of the Foleshill factory, with that characteristic timber style, it also proves that SS Cars Ltd and the Swallow Coachbuilding Company both had registered offices at that address.

So many styling details used in the SS100 were also found, or developed, in the Mk IV saloons which followed, not least those colossal Lucas headlamps and the 'fencers' grille' horns.

The first few deliveries were made at Olympia Show time, but during the winter SS had to buckle down to the most important job it had ever tackled. Not only was the workforce building its first-ever four-door saloon, it was also facing the task of assembling cars from the bare chassis stage, instead of accepting complete rolling chassis from Standard.

The bodyshell at least was to be constructed by methods familiar to SS, for the shell was based on a wooden skeleton using seasoned ash which was clothed in pressed steel panels, many of which were supplied by the nearby Motor Panels Ltd business, which was also in Whitmore Park.

The first independent road test of the 2½-litre saloon (registered BRW 34) appeared in *The Autocar* in April 1936, a special issue most appropriately placarded as the 'Spring Number'. While we must remember that *The Autocar* and *The Motor* always tried to

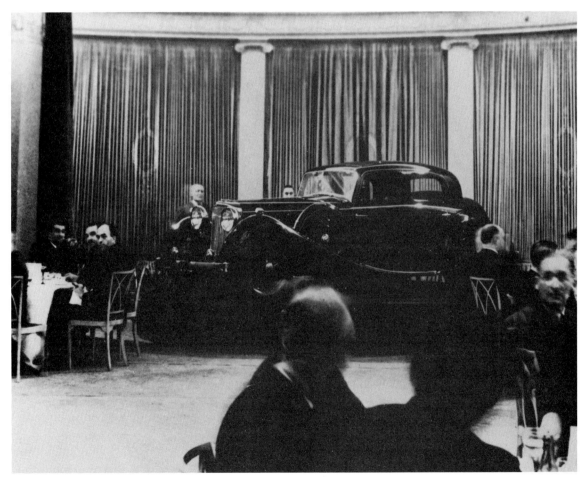

This famous picture was taken at the unveiling of the original 2½-litre SS-Jaguar, at the Mayfair Hotel in September 1935. The lines of this car were only slightly modified for the 'all-steel' models, including a new 3½-litre version, which went on sale in 1937/1938, continuing in production until the late 1940s.

SS-Jaguar – the Market-Place in 1936

Although the two new SS-Jaguars offered remarkable value when they went on sale in 1935, in Britain they faced a good deal of competition from other long-established makes. This was a selection of the obvious rivals to the new 2½-litre model at Olympia Show in October 1935:

Make/Model	Engine size cc	UK Price*
SS-Jaguar 2½-litre	2,663	£385
Alvis Silver Eagle	2,362	£598
Alvis Crested Eagle	2,762	£800
MG '2-litre' SA	2,288	£375
Riley Adelphi V8	2,178	£450
Riley Kestrel V8	2,178	£450
Triumph Gloria	1,991	£395
Wolseley 21hp	2,916	£340

SS in fact found itself on sure ground because cars like the Alvis, which offered as much performance, were much more expensive, while those like the MG SA and the Triumph Gloria were much less powerful and not nearly as rapid. The MG was arguably as attractive as the SS-Jaguar (Cecil Kimber, like William Lyons, had a good styling 'eye'), and the Triumph had great charm, but buyers wanted acceleration too.

* In those days, there were no taxes to be added to the factory's quoted price.

---

one-way speed being 88.24mph (142km/h): the car could reach 69mph (111km/h) in third and 46mph (74km/h) in second gear. Although such tests were not nearly as detailed as they were to become in post-war years, we also know that the 0–60mph sprint was achieved in 17.4 seconds. Overall fuel consumption was on the high side at 21mpg (13.5l/100km), for this was a substantial car weighing in at 3,376lb (1,531kg).

The testers, led by H.S. Linfield and Douglas Clease, positively fawned over the machine:

> Many people regarded the SS-Jaguar as being one of the outstanding cars in the last Olympia Show, bearing in mind the reputation which the makers have already built up for a smart and distinctive car possessing an excellent performance and the remarkably good value in its class this new model, the Jaguar, gave every appearance of offering.

Maybe there could have been improvements in grammar, but the general sense was clear! There was a lot more in the same vein:

> The performance is worthy of the appearance and comes up to expectations. The Jaguar is intended to appeal to those who want a sports car performance, and thus undoubtedly is provided.... It is steady in the sports car manner on corners, can be put fast with complete confidence into an open road curve, yet is not harsh on the springing, the back seat as well as the front seat occupants riding very comfortably.
>
> The whole finish, both inside and outside, is extremely well done, with very good leather and attractively polished woodwork used for the instrument board and cappings ....

It was the final summing-up, however, which set the seal on this test:

write nice things about British cars in those days, there was no doubt that they enjoyed driving this car, taking it all the way down to the West Country and back, before checking performance figures on the Brooklands race track.

The headline to this test quoted: 'New Overhead Valve Model Gives an Exceptional Performance on test: Appearance which Belies its Actual Price'. The mean maximum speed was 85.71mph (138km/h), the best

From experience of it over a comprehensive distance, taking in a wide variety of conditions with loads varying from the driver alone up to full capacity, this SS-Jaguar does even better than one might anticipate. It is not too much to say that it is a credit to the British automobile industry, and seems almost unbelievably good at the price, which is not meant to be in any way a reflection upon it.

Bolstered by this and similar laudatory reports from other sources, SS set about building as many cars as possible. A total of 1,720 cars were built in 1935, 'pre-Jaguar', as it were, but 2,469 cars were produced in

This was the sort of competition Jaguar had to face in the late 1930s – a 2.5-litre Daimler DB18 sports saloon, this particular car as prepared for The Autocar's *'Sammy' Davis to drive in the 1939 Monte Carlo rally. SS-Jaguar's major advantage over cars like this was that its cars were invariably much cheaper and much more powerful than their competitors.*

Several Jaguar generations in the same photograph, which was taken in the early 1980s to celebrate the 60th anniversary of the setting up of Swallow Coachbuilding. Sir William Lyons, by this time retired from business, with Jaguar's 1980s Chief Executive John Egan, poses in front of the ex-Lady Lyons 2½-litre SS-Jaguar saloon, and a 1983 model Jaguar XJ6.

1936 and no fewer than 3,554 would follow in 1937. The 1936–37 financial year, which ended on 31 July, realized a profit of no less than £34,292 – which in crude terms was about £10 per car. This sounds paltry today, but was certainly enough to keep the company expanding.

Modifications and improvements were always being made to the cars in this period, as Lyons strove to drive costs down while keeping quality up, and to increase his sales. The old-type SSI and SSII models were dropped in 1936, while the four-seater 2½-litre Tourer would not survive long in 1937.

For 1937 the 2½-litre's peak power was squeezed up to 104bhp, there were changes to the steering, the shock absorbers, the springs themselves, the brakes, the seats, the windscreen wipers, the instrument panel layout, the window ventilation etc. As already noted, Lyons was restless, rarely satisfied, and always trying to make improvements – especially if this could be done without increasing costs.

This, though, was the time when the first truly 'big-engined' Jaguar began to take shape. Not only was a new type of body construction and a new drop-head coupé style being developed, but a more powerful, 3½-litre engine, was on the way.

2 The 3½-Litre: Pre-War Elegance, Post-War Success

Before introducing the 3½-litre and tracing its development, I would like to quote from an earlier book I wrote on the Jaguar XJ6:

> Nothing is more important to the launch of a new car than its ancestry. If the new model has no heritage, no tradition, no breeding or – in horse-racing terms – no 'form', it has an uphill struggle to be accepted.
>
> If it comes from a well-known stable, on

the other hand, it is likely to be given a good reception even before the critics get behind the wheel.

Thirty years before the XJ6 was launched, the same sentiments applied to the first of the truly rapid, large-engined, Jaguars. It had taken only two years for SS to establish the SS-Jaguar as a formidable new marque and sales were increasing rapidly. Now SS

The shape of the first post-war Jaguars was established with the 'all-steel' SS-Jaguars of 1937–9. This contemporary study of a pre-war car not only shows off the car's sensuous lines, but the lady model also emphasizes how relatively low the roof line was.

planned to complete the range with an even larger version – a 3.5-litre engined car.

But that was not all. At this stage in SS's history, changes and improvements were being made every model year and sometimes more frequently than that. This meant that although the 3½-litre was scheduled for introduction in September 1937, it was only one of a number of far-reaching changes planned for that time. At the same time SS-Jaguar was also proposing to fit all its cars with a brand-new design of chassis frame, along with an all-steel version of the existing body style. If this wasn't an ambitious enough programme on its own, problems with new facilities meant the changeover from 1937-model to 1938-model assembly was delayed by months. Orders taken at the Earls Court Motor Show in October 1937 could not in fact be satisfied until the spring of 1938!

GROWING PAINS

By 1937 William Lyons could see that his existing factory was rapidly running out of space. Simple assembly lines laid down in 1935, to accommodate chassis assembly and SS-Jaguar bodyshell production, were already at capacity – there were times when more than eighty cars a week were being built – and the body shop was bursting at the seams. Not only that, but it was clear that the old SSI-based chassis frame was overdue for change.

The major problem was in the body shop, where SS's traditional building methods – producing a wooden skeleton on which to assemble steel body panels – had reached their limits. Ever since 1928/9, when Swallow had arrived from Blackpool, bodyshells had been manufactured in the same way, a method which had evolved over the years in the motor industry. Starting with blocks of seasoned ash, wooden frame members were shaped by cutting, milling, planing, and gouging. Individual members were then slotted together in jigs, glued, screwed and bolted together in a process which took a great deal of time, space and manpower.

Bravely, therefore, Lyons decided to go one step further towards matching the major car producers. Instead of using a wooden framework on which to pin the steel panels, he would use an all-steel shell instead, where welding took the place of pins and where little craftsman-like adjustment would be required. This, at least, was the theory. The change, it was thought, could be made without major alterations to the styling and wherever possible the modern design would continue to use existing pressings from the wooden-framed SS-Jaguar saloons; in the event, few of these remained.

For larger concerns, this decision could have been turned into action merely by spending a lot of money, by calling up Pressed Steel or Fisher and Ludlow and letting them take the strain. But not with SS. The problem was not only that SS had never had steel-pressing facilities of its own, but that it had never before used an all-steel bodyshell. At a time when demand was booming, and when the independent bodyshell producers were taking on lots of new business, SS had no track record to assure them of immediate attention. When enquiries were made of Pressed Steel, not only did that company quote a lengthy (twelve months at least) period for body tooling, but they also wanted well in excess of £50,000 for the jigging required.

Lyons therefore took a big decision which, as it transpired, was to bring unforeseen problems to his company. SS, he decided, would have to assemble its own bodies, using pressings bought in from outside specialists. SS would clear out all the old-fashioned wood-framing jigs to make space for steel assembly facilities. So far, so good, but this seems to have been where inexperience suddenly cost the company dear. What seems to have happened is that a prototype shell was styled and engineered, after which (to quote fellow historian Paul Skilleter on this point): 'few drawings were made – instead, patterns and templates were taken direct from a prototype shell and then despatched to the various firms who were to produce the individual parts'.

Each of the chosen sub-contractors – Pressed Steel of Cowley, Motor Panels (from next door!), Rubery Owen (from Darlaston) and Sankeys of Wellington – was expert in its field, but somehow this policy of dispersion fell apart right away. When panels began to arrive to be assembled to a pre-production body, it was found that they did not match each other. Details of the problem are now lost in the mists of history, but because few drawings existed, it wasn't easy to work out which pressings were correct and which were faulty. Suffice to say that much aggravation, modification, scrapping of shells and lead loading of welded joints was needed before acceptable shells were being built.

SIMILAR BUT DIFFERENT

For 1938 Bill Heynes, this time with plenty of time to think about it, had developed a completely new chassis frame, even more rigid, with totally box-section wide members and three sturdy cross-members, but without the cruciform (X-member) pressings of the old SSI-based design.

Still catering for half-elliptic springs and beam axles front and rear, it was an altogether more integrated and technically elegant layout than before, and was claimed to be 30 per cent stiffer in torsion than the 1937 variety. The rear axle was 2in (5cm) wider than before – the track of the six-cylinder cars had been increased to 56in

(142cm) — and still carried shock absorbers on brackets on the axle, rather than on the chassis frame. As before, the chassis frame passed under the line of the back axle, and the rear springs were mounted inboard of the main members, rather than under it, as was more conventional for this period.

For the six-cylinder cars the wheelbase was 120in (3,048mm), and for the four-cylinder 1½-litre car it was to be 112.5in (2,857mm), 4.5in (114mm) longer than for the old-type 1½-litre. Although its beam axle layout would be technically obsolete by the time it was superseded in 1948, this frame did a good, trouble-free job for SS-Jaguar/Jaguar for a decade.

Visually, the four-door saloon shell itself was similar to that of the obsolete wooden-framed 1937 design, but was different in many ways. Not only was the internal structure in steel pressings, the wheelbase slightly longer at 120in (3,048mm) (that dimension would never again be changed on 'Big Jaguars' – it had a life of thirty-two years), and the rear track 2in (5cm) wider, but the cabin itself was rather more roomy being wider and longer.

The immediate way to 'pick' one shell from the other is to point out that the all-steel style had a greater rake to the front A-pillar joint (where the front door met the scuttle). However, in its technical analysis of the new style, *The Autocar* pointed out that:

Dealing first with the new coachwork, the primary objective has been to increase the available room and to render entry and exit more easy. The new bodies are much wider than were the previous models, and incidentally look, in the rear view, more sumptuous as a result.

Slight changes in the position of mounting and in the construction have added about five inches to the interior length. Thus the rear doors become considerably wider ...

Another point is that the forward edge of the front slopes in line with the windscreen angle.

This again provides a wider door, and the opening at the base gives a great deal more leg room for getting in and out ... In actual fact these changes in the saloon design have a much greater effect than a plain description might suggest, for they have obliterated any suggestion of a 'sports saloon' ... Despite these changes the outward appearance of the Jaguar has not suffered in the least.

Comparing the diagrams published in *The Autocar* road tests of 1936 and 1939, for the 'wood' and the 'steel' bodyshells respectively, it is easy to see where the gains had been placed. Although the car itself was no wider than before, it was 8in (203mm) longer overall at 186in (4,724mm) instead of 178in (4,521mm). The rear seat cushion was 5in (120mm) wider, each of the front bucket seats was 2in (50mm) wider and there was significantly more front and rear leg room. For the owner-driver, it was nice to see that the front door gap had been increased from 23.5in (600mm) to 27in (690mm).

At the time of its launch, little was made of a new body option, a smart and spacious two-door drop-head coupé type available with all three engine/chassis specifications. Ahead of the screen this was identical with the new saloons, but aft of that there were large rear-hinged doors. Because of the smaller numbers likely to be built, and the peculiar problems in making such bodies rigid enough, a certain amount of wood still figured in the construction.

The fold-back hood, complete with 'sexy' external irons, not only had copious horse-hair padding to give it a smooth shape, but there was also a separate internal headlining. The whole assembly folded back to be covered by a separate envelope and if necessary the car could run in what is known as

the *coupe de ville* position, where only the section above the front seats had been retracted. This luxurious soft-top, incidentally, featured a tiny rear window, but no one seemed to complain about that.

The trim, detailing and furnishing of the new cars was as impressive as expected, with wood, leather trim and carpet well in evidence. The nose was as impressive as ever, with vast and magnificent Lucas P100 headlamps, chrome-grilled horns and extra driving lamps with the leaping-Jaguar mascot available as an extra for two guineas (£2.20).

When you consider other features which were standard – which included the adjustable-length steering column, the opening windscreen, the rear window anti-dazzle blind and the impressive display of tools all mounted inside the drop-down boot lid, it was a miracle that SS-Jaguar could sell cars at such low prices. One reason, of course, was that high-quality materials were only used where they were on show, another was that the keenest possible purchase prices were always negotiated and yet another was that Lyons was totally dedicated to a lack of wastage in all departments.

NEW ENGINES

For enthusiasts, the biggest talking point was the engine line-up. Not only was there a brand-new 3.5-litre six-cylinder unit, but SS-Jaguar had made more improvements to the existing 'six', and for the first time there was to be a new overhead-valve '1½-litre' four-cylinder unit as well.

The 1½-litre unit, in fact, was nothing of the sort, but actually a 1.8-litre. In fact it was a Weslake overhead-valve conversion (like that of the existing 'six') on the basis of the existing Standard Flying Fourteen unit of 1,776cc. As ever, Standard manufactured

A great deal of wood was still used in building up the body of this derivative of the design. The extra driving lamps on TMH 964 are non-standard, being Lucas accessories of the 1950s/1960s period.

this engine for SS-Jaguar, though at first their agreement with Lyons did not allow its use in Standard products. It would not be until 1946 that this engine appeared on Standard-built cars – these being the post-war Triumph 1800 Roadster, and Town and Country models.

The 2½-litre engine for 1938 featured small changes, including a higher compres-sion ratio and large SU carburettors, but these changes were quite overshadowed by the launch of the new 3½-litre unit, which was guaranteed to provide the SS-Jaguar saloon with a top speed of at least 90mph (145km/h).

Except in detail, the 3½-litre engine looked like the 2½-litre, being a direct 'stretched' development of it, for the basic

Hood up or hood down, the drophead coupé version of the 1937–1948 SS-Jaguar was an attractive machine. The soft-top was fully padded, and when erect turned this car into a wind-proof, if rather claustrophobic, closed car.

cast-iron Standard cylinder block featured seven main crankshaft bearings and was very robust. It needed to be, for power outputs of this magnitude had certainly never been envisaged when Standard started designing these engines at the end of the 1920s.

To achieve the new 3,485cc capacity, both bore *and* stroke had had to be increased. The 2½-litre used 73mm x 106mm, these also being the same dimensions employed in the side-valve Standard Flying 20 of the period, while the 3½-litre used 82mm x

110mm, both being unique to this unit. That bore increase of 9mm was absolutely the largest which the existing cylinder block layout could accept, which no doubt explains why a slightly longer stroke was also needed to provide the required capacity.

With 1.5in (38mm) SU carburettors and a 7.2:1 compression ratio, this Weslake-inspired engine developed a stirring 125bhp at 4,500rpm, a figure which made many other British car-makers very jealous indeed! It was the sort of power output which turned the SS-Jaguar 3½-litre model

The only easy way to identify the 1½-litre version of this range was to spot that the smaller four-cylinder engine only needed a shorter wheelbase and set of bonnet pressings to accommodate it.

into a formidable high-speed model of its day. A top speed of 90mph (145km/h) may sound pedestrian today, but by late-1930s standards this was a very exciting machine to drive and own – and all at a remarkably low price.

In an account like this, gearboxes tend to be ignored, so I should make it clear that the four-speed slow-synchromesh type of box, of the sort we would come to know so intimate-ly in the post-war years, had already become established. SS-Jaguar, of course, had no gear cutting machinery of its own, so had to buy in the gearboxes. At this time Standard was producing them, complete with the neat remote control extension, but in later years Moss Gear of Birmingham would take over manufacture.

This, then, is where the story of the 'Big Jaguars' really begins, so it is appropriate to list SS-Jaguar's complete 1938-model line-up:

Model	Power (bhp)	UK Price
1½-litre saloon	65	£298
1½-litre drop-head coupé	65	£318
2½-litre saloon	105	£395
2½-litre drop-head coupé	105	£415
3½-litre saloon	125	£445
3½-litre drop-head coupé	125	£465
SS100 – 2½-litre	105	£395
SS100 – 3½-litre	125	£445

THE PRE-WAR CARS

Although the 3½-litre model was unveiled in September 1937, very few cars were delivered before March 1938. Then, with body assembly problems solved, the floodgates opened. By April 1938 between 85 and 100 SS-Jaguars of all types were being produced every week, this figure rising to 120 a week by June. Even so, it is only fair to say that although the 3½-litre was the most desirable of the new range, it was not the fastest-selling. That honour always went to the much slower 1½-litre model, for not only was that car significantly cheaper, but it cost a lot less to tax.

These days we tend to forget that annual taxation was a flat rate levied according to a car's official 'RAC Horsepower' rating. This was a somewhat nebulous assessment based on a car engine's piston area. Naturally this favoured small-engined cars, particularly those with narrow bores and longer strokes. In 1937 the RAC Rating was 15s (75p) per listed horsepower, and the SS-Jaguars lined up as follows:

Model	hp rating	Annual tax
1½-litre	13.2	£10 10s
2½-litre	19.8	£15
3½-litre	25.01	£18 15s

When you consider that costs have risen at least thirty-fold by the mid-1990s, you will realize why large-engined cars sometimes struggled to sell. At 1995 values, this means that you were being asked to pay the equivalent of about £550 merely to licence a car!

By this time the motoring press had started its love affair with SS-Jaguar, so when *The Autocar* tested a 3½-litre saloon in April 1939, the superlatives flowed. Reporting on a £445 car which reached nearly 90mph (145km/h), testers wrote:

Since the introduction of the Jaguar models some two years ago the SS has been an outstanding make from the point of view of performance in relation to price, also a car of unusually pleasing appearance ...

It is decidedly in that category of a 'driver's car', for there is that ready response to the throttle pedal to satisfy anyone who likes to send the speedometer needle soaring on main roads, and it handles well too ....

Here, though, the different standards of the 1930s became clear:

Somewhere around 60mph is reached almost automatically on sufficiently clear roads, and between 60 and 70 is the natural maintainable pace.

The Motor's Sports Editor, Rodney Walkerley, who liked to be thought of as a humorous character – he certainly wrote like one – ran a 3½-litre for business and pleasure at this time. Among other observations he made in print was:

The amusing thing is that at such a small outlay [£445] you can take on anything on the road. The car goes so fast that I have been too lazy to bother about checking the speedometer ... once, on that back leg of the Rheims circuit, which starts with a downhill rush and goes level for the rest, it did 96mph, and held it, three up and with luggage.

Although the ride was undoubtedly firm, and the steering heavy at low speeds, the latest SS-Jaguars were well up to accepted standards, as Walkerley confirmed:

> The road-holding, of course, is famous. No need for me to talk about how the car corners and handles generally as a sports car should, although this is a full five-seater touring saloon and by no means a racer ....

From every tester there was more in the same vein and if the road tax imposed had not been so high many more sales would surely have been achieved.

Few changes were made to the cars for

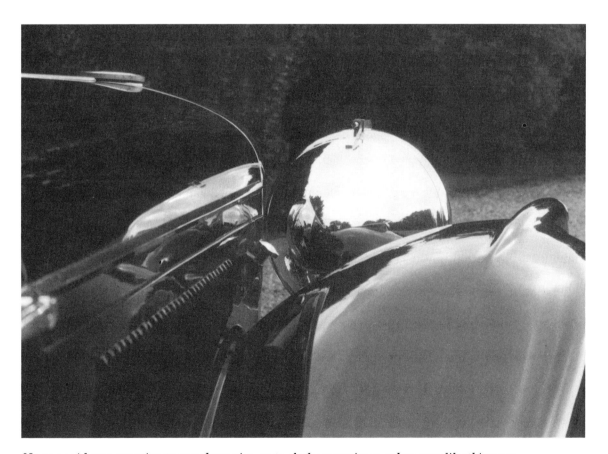

No one paid any attention to aerodynamics, or to sleek convenience, when cars like this were designed in the late 1930s. The chrome knob had to be unscrewed to release the bonnet catches, the bonnet then had to be lifted carefully – how many cars like this have you seen with damaged wing panels, or scratches on the opening bonnet panels themselves?

1939 and in spite of the looming political crisis in Europe, the British government's rush to re-arm its military forces and the hefty increase in motoring taxation which followed, SS-Jaguar sales soared yet again in 1939, with 200 cars a week now being squeezed out of limited space at the Foleshill factory.

For 1940 SS-Jaguar made only evolutionary changes to the trim and furnishing of the saloons, and only minor improvements to the chassis. However, there was one important innovation to the saloons which was to fit them with what was called 'air-conditioning'. In truth, this was only a simple fresh-air heater/ventilator (and, in a Jaguar tradition which was to continue for many years, it really didn't work very well!), but it certainly gave Lyons what the advertising industry would later call a 'unique selling proposition'.

Quite simply, at this time, no other British car – not even a Rolls-Royce – was fitted with a heater as standard, so the 1940-model SS-Jaguars were truly setting the pace. Up to that time, the only way to keep warm in a car during cold weather was to wrap up well, wear a hat and gloves and (for the passengers, if not the driver) to use a travelling rug.

This explains why the motoring press went over the top in its description of the installation, which relied on fresh air from a scuttle-mounted vent and hot water from a valve on the engine. For Lyons, however, all this endeavour was made in vain. The 1940 models were revealed in *The Autocar* of 28 July 1939. Six weeks later the nation was at war.

SS-JAGUAR AT WAR

During the winter of 1939/40 SS-Jaguar private-car assembly ran down very quickly indeed, with only 899 cars being produced

after 1 August 1939. This gave a grand total for all SS-Jaguar types of 1935–40 (including SS100s) of 14,313 cars. As rapidly as possible the factories were turned over to production, development and testing of military machinery, and all thought of private-car innovation had to be abandoned.

Although the factory building originally erected in Swallow Road to produce Avro Manchester aircraft (the predecessor of the famous Lancaster) was never used for that purpose, it was soon filled with other contracts and yet another building was eventually set up to tackle all the work.

In the next six years the factories produced aircraft components in profusion, parts for aircraft engines, for guns, and an amazing variety of trailers and sidecars. One result was that a flood of new machine tools was installed (SS-Jaguar had always been poorly equipped up until that time) and as the author can testify, these were tools which, in some cases, would still be found dotted around the Jaguar machine shops fifty years later.

In this period, the design team eventually took the opportunity to get down to some serious study of new cars and engines for the peace which would surely follow – but that particular story belongs to the next two chapters.

Although there was some bomb damage in 1940, which was quickly repaired, the company was poised to turn back to making cars as soon as the war had been won. Because of the abhorrent war-time connotations of the 'SS' initials, Lyons made haste to drop them from his company titles. From March 1945 the parent company became 'Jaguar Cars Ltd' and all post-war cars would henceforth be called Jaguars.

In the meantime, further corporate upheavals had taken place. Having taken control of Motor Panels Ltd just before the war, Lyons found himself short of capital in 1945 and reluctantly decided to sell that company. Rubery Owen were the new purchasers. Jaguar's chance to be independent of outside bodyshell suppliers had gone and would not be regained until the mid-1980s when it took control of the Castle Bromwich premises.

Jaguar had also simplified its relations with the Standard Motor Company, where all its engines had previously been manufactured. Although he was much too much of a gentleman to spell it out, Lyons was heartily relieved by this, for he had always found it difficult to deal with the dictatorial John Black, who had been knighted for his wartime efforts.

Standard had taken control of the 'Triumph' marque at the end of 1944, though not of the factory down Swallow Road, which had been taken over by the British government for production of Claudel-Hobson aircraft carburettors. Then, as Lyons's successor, Alick Dick, once told me:

> Bill Lyons wanted to buy the tooling from us [for the Jaguar engine] – he wanted to make all of his Jaguars in the future – and John Black was willing to let him have that so that we could build a competitive car. We kept the four-cylinder tooling, but it just wasn't viable without a new chassis and a new name. So that's why we bought Triumph ….

Later in life (in 1969, when he read the Lord

From 1945 'SS-Jaguar' became 'Jaguar', the proudly detailed radiator badge being modified to suit.

Wakefield Gold Medal Paper) Sir William Lyons filled in the rest of the story:

> Sir John Black told me that he would no longer be able to make our engine, and after some discussion offered to sell us the special plant he had put down for its production – very generously at the written-down value.
>
> Before the end of the war, Black had given me reason for a great deal of anxiety on the question of the exclusive continuity of the engine he was making for us. Several other makers had asked him to supply them, and I had not found it easy to prevent him from doing so, even though he accepted that the design of the engine, apart from the cylinder block and crankcase, was ours. Therefore, I was delighted to learn of his proposals as I felt it was a release from an arrangement which I could not have broken honourably, having regard for the fact that it was his willingness to put down the plant, which we could not afford at the time, that got us off the ground with this new engine. I saw this move as a great step towards our becoming the self-contained manufacturing unit at which I aimed.
>
> I had a great admiration for John Black in many respects, but I quickly grasped the opportunity to obtain security. Therefore, within a few days, I sent transport to collect the plant, and sent our cheque in payment for it.
>
> It turned out that I had been right to do so for it was not long before Black proposed that we should revert to the previous arrangement and return the plant to Standard ... He pressed me very hard, even to the extent of suggesting that we should form a separate company together ....

Accordingly, from 1945 Jaguar was much more of a manufacturing (as opposed to assembly) business than ever before. For the first time it would be manufacturing six-cylinder engines within its own walls (in an area originally allocated to repairing Whitley bombers), though the four-cylinder engines would continue to be produced by Standard and would also be fitted to the new Triumph 1800 Roadster and Saloon models of the 1946–9 period, but never to any Standard-badged cars.

POST-WAR JAGUARS: EVOLUTION, NOT REDESIGN

As soon as war-time contracts could be wound up, Lyons set his team to re-establishing Jaguar as a producer of private cars, and the very first post-war models were assembled in July 1945. With the exception that the SS100 sports cars had been dropped, along with the 1½-litre - drop-head coupé model, there were no major changes to the line-up. Retrospectively, and for very tenuous reasons, these cars would later become known as 'Mk IVs'.

Since the Government had made it clear that most cars would have to be exported if supplies of sheet steel were to be guaranteed, Bill Heynes's design team made sure that left-hand steering would soon be available (but supplies were not ready until mid-1947) and for the first two or three years very few cars were actually delivered to UK customers.

Technically and visually, there were some improvements, none of them obvious to the showroom visitor – though, if they looked carefully, they would have seen 'Jaguar' on the hub caps, where 'SS' had previously featured. Hypoid bevel rear axles from Salisbury (instead of ENV spiral bevel assemblies) were fitted to six-cylinder Jaguars, while many engines were fitted with low-compression cylinder heads. This was especially true of UK-market examples, where cars were obliged to use the awful

On the Mk IV Jaguars, access to the engine was good by contemporary standards, but the two-piece fold-up bonnet had to be removed completely for major repair work to be carried out. Fuel pumps (close to the cylinder head) got rather hot in torrid weather conditions. Note the strange profile of the two exhaust manifolds, shapes made necessary by the close proximity of the bulkhead.

Imposing from any angle, the original Jaguar-based 3½-litre model was one of the very last to be built, and was registered in 1949.

low-octane war-time grade called 'Pool'. The major change, however, was to selling prices. War-time inflation, along with the introduction of Purchase Tax, had caused prices to rocket. Here is a comparison between Jaguar prices of September 1939, and September 1945:

Total retail price	September 1939	September 1945
1½-litre saloon	£298	£684
2½-litre saloon	£395	£889
3½-litre saloon	£445	£991

Demand for the latest Jaguars was colossal, so waiting lists (especially in the UK) stretched to years and there was no way that every potential sale could be met. However, even though the Jaguar factory's trim stores suffered a serious fire in January 1947 and there was a nationwide shortage of coal and electricity in the same year, the company pushed up production as soon as possible. In the year ending 31 July 1947 3,393 cars were built (which was the same as that achieved ten years earlier), while drophead coupés finally came back at the end of 1947.

Jaguar 3½-litre (1945–9)

Numbers built
1,309 pre-war (+ 5,403 2½-litre pre-war)
4,420 post-war (+ 1,861 2½-litre post-war)

Layout
Box-section chassis frame with separate steel bodyshell. Five-seater, front engine/rear drive, sold as four-door saloon, or drop-head coupé

Engine
Type	Jaguar (previously SS-Jaguar) ohv
Block material	Cast iron
Head material	Cast iron
Cylinders	6 in-line
Cooling	Water
Bore and stroke	82 x 110mm
Capacity	3,485cc
Main bearings	7
Valves	2 per cylinder, pushrod and rocker operation
Compression ratio	6.6:1 or 7.2:1
Carburettors	2 SU 1.5in
Max. power	125bhp @ 4,500rpm
Max. torque	184lb/ft @ 2,000rpm

Transmission
Four-speed manual gearbox, with synchromesh on top, third and second gears

Clutch	Single dry plate; mechanically operated

Internal gearbox ratios
Top	1.00
3rd	1.34
2nd	1.94
1st	3.37
Reverse	3.37
Final drive	4.27:1

Suspension and steering
Front	Beam axle, half-elliptic leaf springs, hydraulic lever-arm dampers
Rear	Live (beam) axle, by half-elliptic leaf springs, hydraulic lever-arm dampers
Steering	Worm-and-nut
Tyres	5.50-18in cross-ply
Wheels	Centre-lock, wire-spoke
Rim width	4.5in

Brakes

Type	Drum brakes at front and rear, hydro-mechanically operated
Size	14in diameter drums

Dimensions (in/mm)

Track	
Front	54/1,372
Rear	56/1,422
Wheelbase	120/3,048
Overall length	186/4,724
Overall width	66/1,676
Overall height	61/1,549
Unladen weight	3,668lb/1,663kg

Other models :

The 1½-litre and 2½-litre models were closely related.

1½-litre This used the same basic chassis/style, but on a 112.5in/2,858mm wheelbase. The four-cylinder engine measured 73 x 106mm, 1,776cc. With a 7.6:1 compression ratio, peak power was 65bhp @ 4,600rpm.

2½-litre This used the same chassis/style, on the same 120in/3,048mm wheelbase. The six-cylinder engine measured 73mm x 106mm, 2,663cc. With a 7.6:1 compression ratio, peak power was 105bhp @ 4,600rpm.

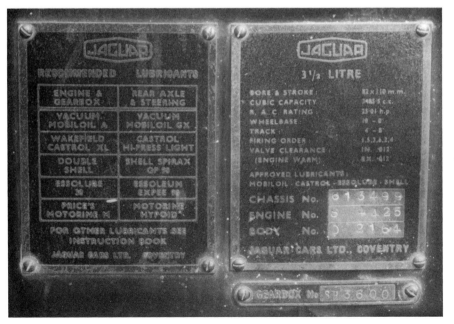

This under-bonnet plate on Anne Lewis's 'Mk IV' not only lists all the relevant identification numbers, but reminds the owner of the wheelbase, track, engine dimensions and firing order. It also lists the various makes of lubrication recommended when the car was built.

The spare wheel on 'Mk IV' models was stowed neatly under the floor of the boot, and accessible through a swivelling flap in the tail.

Even in the current Jaguar range, 1990s cars don't come as well equipped these days! The late 1940s Jaguar had a hinge-down boot lid whose cover lifted to reveal a comprehensive tool kit. Very few restored examples have a full set – Mrs Anne Lewis's 3½-litre is a rare exception.

By 1948, however, Britain's motor industry was nearly ready to unveil a flood of post-war cars. Somehow, war-time damage had been repaired, factories had been converted fully to peace-time operations and ways had been found around most post-war shortages. Although Lyons did not boast of forthcoming new cars, the erstwhile SS-Jaguars were beginning to show their age. The original style, of course, was now thirteen years old, the beam-axle chassis design was obsolete and the cabin of these sports saloons was beginning to look a little cramped. Even so, there were features of these thoroughbred Jaguars which rival concerns could not match, notably the high level of fittings, the style, the quality of fixtures and fittings and the performance, which was quite outstanding for the price asked.

The successor to these fine cars, the Mk V, was launched at Britain's first post-war Motor Show – Earls Court in October 1948, but this was still not quite the end for the old-shape machines. Even though they had been previewed in October, the first deliveries of Mk Vs were not made until March 1949.

It is a measure of the old Mk IV's appeal that it was still in demand after its successor had been launched and sales continued for six months in the winter of 1948/1949.

Unlike modern saloon shells, that of the late-1940s Jaguar was built up from a multitude of small pressings and a great deal of lead-loading; painstaking finishing was needed to get this smooth effect into the showroom car.

It was this sort of attention to decorative detail which made post-war Jaguars such delightful machines to study and to own. William Lyons spent a great deal of time getting every detail to his satisfaction.

With the exception of the Jaguar Driver's Club badge, this 1949 3½-litre model was still totally original when photographed in 1994. Those wonderful Lucas headlamps are virtually unobtainable these days.

So easy to damage, so difficult to restore! Lucas 'Trafficators' seem to be a dying breed these days – one unwise knock on those hinges could put the entire door alignment at risk.

Attention all restorers! This is how a properly rebuilt 'Mk IV' should look inside the cabin. Note the way the rev counter needle is arranged to pivot anti-clockwise as revs built up and the trim patterns of the seats.

Compared with the pre-war cars, post-war 3½-litre models had very plain door trim panel styles.

When the Mk IV was dropped, so was the four-cylinder Jaguar. Although it had always sold faster than the six-cylinder types, the 1½-litre was by no means a quick car. It did not fit in with Lyons's vision of 100mph (160km/h) Jaguars so both he and Standard (which built the engines) were happy to see it go.

After that, the assembly lines were finally cleared to make way for the Mk V. Total post-war production was 11,952, of which a mere 664 were 2½-litre or 3½-litre drop-head coupés – not quite up to pre-war levels, but achieved in a shorter time. Now it was time for the Mk V to take over. Would it be as much of a success?

3 Mk V: Modern Chassis and Traditional Style

In an ideal business world, Jaguar would never have needed to make the Mk V. Even before the end of the war, William Lyons had laid down his strategy for the future – which was to see a new 100mph (160km/h) saloon car put on to the market. If a new bodyshell and in particular if the brand-new XK engine had been ready earlier, the Mk V would never have appeared.

In the late 1940s the obstacles facing thrusting businessmen were enormous. After the war, Britain's motor industry need-ed time to re-equip. Buildings which had been used during the previous six years to assemble aero engines, bombers, tanks and armoured cars had to be emptied. They needed to be turned back to peace-time oper-ations, with new machinery and to be tooled-up for new products. Like most of the new cars which were being developed, most of that machinery and expertise seemed to be for export only, so it took ages to convert a good idea into a saleable product.

At this point, therefore, it is necessary to jump ahead – briefly – to what became the Mk VII saloon, before returning to the Mk V. According to William Lyons's post-war 'mas-ter plan', as soon as it was humanly possible he wanted to ditch the ageing 'Mk IV' range and introduce completely new cars. In what was a very brave decision – no matter in what era it was conceived, it would always have been brave – he wanted Bill Heynes's team to develop a brand new chassis, a brand new engine and a brand new bodyshell, all at the same time. This would not happen often.

Over 1944/5, when he laid down these guidelines, Lyons thought that the new car could be ready by 1948. But Jaguar and its staff always struggled to meet this deadline. Apart from finding the money, it was simply not possible to get the engine, and in partic-ular the bodyshell, ready by that time.

Mk V – why the name?

There doesn't seem to be any logical reason why Jaguar's new Mk V saloon was called a Mk V. Sir William Lyons never bothered to explain, there are no appropriate company records to consult, and logic really defies a 'count-back' to earlier cars. The fact that post-war 1½-litre/2½-litre/3½-litre models eventually became unofficially known as 'Mk IV' didn't help.

Some sources suggest that the new car took its name from the fifth prototype to use independent front suspension, but I cannot believe that William Lyons would have been so unimaginative.

My personal opinion is that someone, almost certainly Lyons, together with Bill Heynes, decided in 1948 that this was really the fifth generation of SS-Jaguar and Jaguar saloon cars, and gave it an appropriate title. In that case, I guess, we must assume as the earlier 'Marks':

SSI (1931)	The original 'Mk 1'
SSII (1931)	The 'Mk 2'
SS-Jaguar of 1935	The 'Mk III'
The 'all-steel'	
SS-Jaguar/Jaguar	
of 1938–48	The 'Mk IV'

Graceful, spacious and fast, but by 1948 standards the Mk V had a distinctly traditional style. But never mind – William Lyons only ever intended it as an interim model.

Well before the end of 1947, therefore, Lyons took a deep breath, accepted the inevitable delays and turned to the design of an interim car. The new chassis could be made ready, he accepted that the ageing six-cylinder push-rod engines could continue for another few years and once again he faced the need to produce a steel saloon bodyshell 'in house'. The new car, when it came, would be the Mk V and what we now know as the Mk VII would have to come later.

NEW SUSPENSION

The new chassis took shape around a new type of front suspension, one that had been developing slowly at SS-Jaguar for some time. Well before SS-Jaguar private car assembly ended in 1939/40, Bill Heynes's tiny design office had started to develop a new frame around a new front suspension system. The existing 'Mk IV' frame, with beam axles at front and rear, dated from

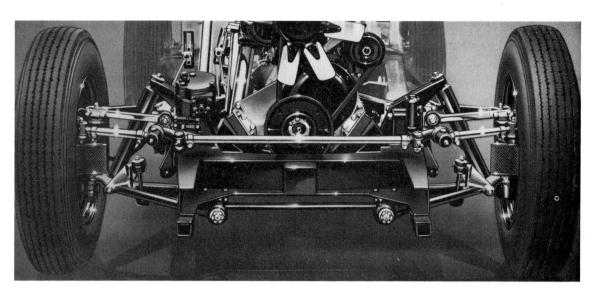

Inspired by the original Citroën traction avant *layout, Jaguar's independent front suspension was designed in 1937, installed in prototype cars well before the Second World War, but not actually put on sale until the Mk V was launched in 1948. In mildly modified form, this would also be used on XK sports cars, E-Types, and Mk VII family models until the 1970s.*

1937/8 and was already technically obsolete, so a new chassis, complete with independent front suspension, would have to be drawn up. There was no question of this being arranged for use under an existing body – the new frame would also be topped by a new body style.

In the 1930s British car-makers had been very slow to adopt independent front ends, even though European car designs were much more advanced at the time. Of the British 'Big Six' neither Ford, Austin nor Vauxhall had ever sold such cars before 1939, while Morris, Standard and the Rootes Group only dabbled with independent front suspension (IFS) on isolated models.

Almost every rival marque in the SS-Jaguar price and size category – Alvis, Armstrong-Siddeley, MG, Riley, Rover, Triumph and Wolseley among them – had stuck to old-fashioned beam-axle chassis throughout the 1930s. Only Daimler/Lanchester, and then only in one case, broke

ranks and went for IFS. Most of these firms, though, were already studying new systems before the outbreak of war.

Bill Heynes had still been working at Rootes when that company first investigated independent suspension systems in the 1930s, but he had not been impressed by the restriction placed upon his department. His work on a new layout for the Hillman Minx came to nothing, while he was also involved in the first primitive Humber 'Evenkeel' independent systems, which used transverse leaf springs and a very unsatisfactory geometry and location. A young Alec Issigonis, too, was also working at Rootes at the time and was apparently involved; like Heynes, he did not like what he was obliged to do.

There was no time to dabble with independent front suspension at SS until 1937/8, when Heynes's inspiration was still the innovative layout of the remarkable front-wheel-drive Citroën *traction avant* model, which had been unveiled in 1934. For this

new monocoque *traction* model, designer
André Lefebvre had chosen a wishbone system sprung on longitudinal torsion bars; it
rigid, well-located, and a technically elegant
system.

Advancing from this layout, Heynes not
only retained longitudinal torsion bars
(which were convenient to 'package' on cars
with a separate chassis frame) but also
incorporated upper and lower ball joints in
the vertical link (or 'stub axle') and
hydraulic telescopic dampers. Although prototype parts for such a suspension system
were soon manufactured, no one found time
to assemble and fit them for road testing.
This was the situation which Walter Hassan
found when he joined SS Cars Ltd as Chief
Experimental Engineer, in place of Laurice
Hathaway, who was moving on to Coventry
Climax.

According to Walter, in his book *Climax in
Coventry:*

> All in all, I doubt if there could have been
> more than half-a-dozen draughtsmen
> involved in mechanical design. My first
> major project at SS was to develop a new
> independent front suspension designed by
> Bill Heynes. When I arrived, the parts had
> been made but were just lying in a heap on
> the workshop floor.
>
> In fact the independent suspension was
> not fitted to a production car, even in modi-
> fied form, until 1948 – on the XK120 and
> the Mk V – because of the break in car pro-
> duction during the war ... Almost as soon as
> war broke out, all car production at SS
> stopped, and we began to make components
> for Armstrong-Siddeley, at the other side of
> Coventry ...

Hassan also made it clear that developing
modern chassis items like this was a really
big step for SS Cars, which was still modest-
ly equipped. Regarding the changeover to
wartime production:

Walter Hassan

The man who started his working life with
Bentley in 1920, and was still dabbling with
new engine developments seventy years
later, had three spells with SS Cars (later
Jaguar Cars), which were bracketed with
an equally illustrious period with Coventry-
Climax. Not only was he a famous engine
designer in post-war years, but he was
equally well known as a racing mechanic
and special car builder in his younger years.

Walter Thomas Frederick Hassan, born
and educated in London, joined Bentley at
Cricklewood as an apprentice, eventually
joined the racing team as a mechanic, and
went on to prepare special cars for Woolf
Barnato and others in the 1930s. After
working briefly at ERA, then at Thomson
and Taylor (at Brooklands), he joined SS
Cars as Chief Development Engineer in
1938, when the 3½-litre model was still new.

Following a brief spell with the Bristol
Aeroplane Company during the war, he
returned to SS in 1943. After dabbling with
the design of lightweight parachute-drop
fighting vehicles, he became a founder
member of the XK engine design and development team, and came to run Jaguar's
busy experimental department when the
Mk V and Mk VII models were being finalized.

In 1950 he became Coventry-Climax's
Chief Engineer, later Technical Director,
where he masterminded the design of racing engines such as the FPE V8, the FPF
four-cylinder, and the FWMV V8 designs.
After Jaguar took over Coventry-Climax in
1963, he found himself with responsibilities
on two sites.

Before returning to Jaguar, full-time, in
1966 as Group Chief Engineer, Power Units,
he was always close to the finalization of the
4.2-litre engines and new transmissions
used in the later Mk X and 420G models.
After taking over from Bill Heynes as
Engineering Director in 1969, he saw the
fabulous V12 engine safely into production,
then finally retired in 1972.

There were a lot of new machines, because in the last year making cars we had survived with very little machinery at all. I remember that I was responsible for bringing the very first lathe into the experimental department, and there were only two old milling machines for making brake-rod fork ends.

Once the basic layout of the new independent front suspension had been settled, and tested on prototype chassis frames hidden under 3½-litre model bodies, the design of what became the Mk V could begin in earnest. Like other important elements of Jaguar post-war models, this was a 'fire-watching special'.

GENESIS IN WARTIME

As every Jaguar enthusiast surely knows, the world-famous twin-ohc XK engine was conceived during Sunday night 'firewatching' sessions at the Foleshill factory. Few realize, however, that it was not only engines, but also chassis and body styles which were also discussed in that legendary period. The XK engine, which made all the headlines in 1948, was only one of the major projects started at this time.

Walter Hassan, so closely involved in everything which was being developed at the time, summed up succinctly in his own autobiography *Climax in Coventry:*

For all of us, a spell of fire-watching was compulsory every week – which meant that we had to spend one night out of bed as unpaid wardens keeping a look-out for incendiary bombs which might drop on the SS factory or on surrounding houses, then raise the alarm and try to do something to minimize the danger.

Fortunately, air raids on Coventry had just about stopped by 1943, so without something interesting to occupy us, these fire-watching sessions would have been a tedious and tiring bore.

But William Lyons, never a man to miss an opportunity, decided that this was a heaven-sent opportunity to get a bit of planning and discussion going when we were not tremendously busy on essential war work. He made sure that the fire-watching team on Sunday nights would include Bill Heynes, Claude Baily, myself and himself, and he turned these sessions into a sort of running 'design seminar' for what SS would do when car production could be resumed after the war.

We would foregather at the works at about 6pm, sign on, and while keeping an eye on the job, as it were, Mr Lyons would then settle down and talk to us about the future. During my first sojourn with SS, I had always found Mr Lyons to be a rather austere sort of man, very formal in his business contacts, although very interested and very interesting on the question of car design. During those Sunday nights, however, he unbent quite a lot, and I think he got to know us much better. Even so, I never heard him call anyone by their Christian name – no one, that is, except for Fred Gardner ...

He was not trained as an engineer, but he had a very clear idea of the kind of car he wanted to sell, and was always very critical of deficiencies in performance, roadholding, suspension, noise and comfort.

In a little development department office at Foleshill, with camp beds rigged up for our use, the first lines were drawn on paper ... Bill Heynes, as Chief Engineer and Technical Director, was in overall command; Bob Knight (another future Technical Director of Jaguar) busied himself with chassis refinements, including the developed version of the torsion-bar independent front suspension I had built in 1938; our Chief Engine Designer was Claude Baily, who had moved over from the Morris

This was the Mk V's rolling chassis, unencumbered by bodywork, showing how a totally flat body floor was made possible.

Engines factory; and I was to be in charge of engine development once we could spend some time on the test beds.

At this time it was much easier to talk and to develop new designs on paper, than it was to get anything made, so until the war was over the new engines, chassis and styles could only exist on paper.

The emphasis, too, was on bringing the brand-new engine family into existence, a task which was sure to take longer than getting Rubery Owen to produce chassis frames to a new design, so nothing further was done until 1946/7. Later on, in any case, once the prototype XK engines were running, Hassan also found himself in charge of developments of all mechanical items too – so there was no time for anyone to get bored at Foleshill.

After choosing a wheelbase of 120in (3,048mm), which was the same as that of the existing 'Mk IV' model, agreeing to use the same hypoid bevel axle as that of the 'Mk IV', and setting on a 56in (142cm) front track (2in (5cm) wider than that of the 'Mk IV'), Heynes and Bob Knight were soon able to settle on the layout of the new frame. Viewed from above, the straight run of the sturdy box-section side members, which in plan view widened as they neared the rear of the car, was obvious, and from any angle the massive cruciform section under the seats proved that Jaguar was looking for strength and rigidity, not light weight.

Apart from the use of torsion-bar/wishbone IFS, the other major change was to sweep the chassis side members over the top of the axle, instead of insinuating them

The Mk V 'exhibition' chassis, as used by Jaguar at the Paris Salon in 1948. This shows how neatly Bill Heynes's team had integrated the old-type overhead-valve engine into the brand-new chassis, which had torsion bar independent front suspension. The steering column support, of course, is only in place for exhibition purposes. The engine, in fact, was almost identical to that used on 3½-litre models produced from 1938 to 1949.

underneath it. Because the previous 'under-slung' frame was inherently more rigid in the vital suspension pick-up areas, this was a controversial change.

However, although the chassis members which swept up and over the back axle compromised bodyshell capacity a little, at least they allowed more up-and-down axle movement. For the first time since 1932, therefore, the company would be able to soften the back end, and not have to face criticism of an over-firm ride.

As ever on a Jaguar, rear suspension was

by half-elliptic leaf springs (which were considerably longer than before, and not nearly as stiff), but this time they were positioned under (rather than inboard of) the chassis side members. Hydraulic lever arm rear dampers, Girling hydraulic drum brakes and low-geared recirculating ball steering (power-assistance was still years away) completed what was a sturdy, if not actually under-engineered, base for the new car.

This chassis, incidentally, was so satisfactory that when a late decision was made to produce a new two-seater sports car for

Compare this Mk V bonnet badge with that of the 'Mk IV' which it replaced. As far as I can see, there were no differences and why change a winning style?

release at the 1948 Earls Court Motor Show, this car – the famous XK120 – was given an 102in (2,591mm) wheelbase frame which, according to Jaguar authority Paul Skilleter, was designed like this:

> A Mk V chassis was commandeered, complete with suspension, brakes and steering, one foot six inches was cut from the length of the centre section, and the 'X' bracing was removed and replaced by a single box section cross member; the frame was also narrowed slightly ....

So much for careful and unhurried development.

If Lyons's 'master plan' had come to fruition by this time, this chassis should have been supporting the brand-new XK engine for which it was really intended, but in the interim for the Mk V the company used developed versions of the old 'Mk IV' types. Having abandoned four-cylinder engines when the 'Mk IV' had stopped being produced, Jaguar chose to use the two overhead-valve six-cylinder engines which had been manufactured at Foleshill since 1945 –

a 102bhp/2,663cc type and a 125bhp/3,485cc type – both these being virtually identical to the sixes used on 'Mk IV' types. The Moss-manufactured four-speed gearbox, too, was like that of its predecessors.

BODY STYLE

Even before the war was over, Lyons had got together with Fred Gardner to begin experimenting with a series of new body styles for the next generation of saloons. The 'Mk IV' shape, itself a development of the original SS-Jaguar style, really dated back to 1935 and was beginning to look old-fashioned Further, its cabin was no longer spacious enough to satisfy current trends. A drophead coupé was also to be developed, but shaping the saloons initially took precedence.

Throughout the work, in which Gardner's craftsmen built several wooden mock-ups – usually what were known as half-bodies, showing only one side of the car – Lyons strove to provide a roomier car with more modern lines, but one which was still quite clearly descended from the well-liked existing Jaguars. At all times, too, he had to remember that Jaguar would have to assemble its own shells, from pressings bought in from outside suppliers.

Like other firms designing cars for the same social class – Riley, Armstrong-Siddeley and Alvis among them – he was not yet ready to take the big step of trying to develop a fully rounded, full-width style, for this was still all very new to him. Evidence of what he tried to do when evolving the XK120 style (which followed on, chronologically, from work on the Mk V) showed that he floundered for a time. Although he had a remarkable flair for knowing what was right, Lyons often took a long time to 'get it right' and he was often frustrated by his own limitations. In the 1950s I remember talking

to craftsmen at Jaguar who had seen the short-lived 'Lyons-storms' which could erupt when something was not working out the way he wanted.

In its profile, the developing Mk V shape was very similar to the cars it would shortly displace, for all experimental versions always had the same graceful 'trademark' sweep of the front wings, the same general rear-wing/rear-quarter profiles and the same 'sausage-shaped' rear window glass. The entire car was 3in (7.5cm) wider and slightly taller than before, but the front grille was wider and looked more squat.

Unhappily, those magnificent Lucas P100 headlamps were no longer available, so instead Lyons took the radical step of using more normal 7in diameter Lucas lamps, which were partly faired into the inner flank of the front wing pressings. Instead of being at bumper level, the auxiliary driving lamps were also positioned much higher, close to the new headlamps.

There was, however, one new styling 'cue', which would be found on many future Jaguars – the outline of the side windows was swept back beyond the shut face of the rear door before curving forward to meet that shut face at waist level; an opening quarter light filled in the important, but compact, area it surrounded.

Another innovation, which would be found on all future separate-chassis Jaguars, was the use of spats over the rear wheels.

This time, too, the door hinging arrangements had been changed. Front doors were still hinged at the rear, on the B/C-pillar (since these could be swept wide open by wind pressure if inadvertently unlatched when the car was moving this layout became known as 'suicide doors'!), but the rear doors were now hinged at their front edges – also on the B/C-pillar – a much more satisfactory arrangement.

Like the old 'Mk IVs', the Mk V shell was entirely assembled from steel foldings and

For thirty years, one of Jaguar's styling traditions was to supply only a small, sausage-shaped, rear window. Glass was expensive, William Lyons was a practical businessman, and in any case he wanted the rear compartment of his cars to be as discreet as possible.

Mk V lighting detail, with lamps much less costly than those fitted to 'Mk IV' types, but equally as effective.

When Jaguar designed the Mk V, it was determined to protect the bodyshell from accident damage, which explains the sturdy double bumpers and the over-riders. As ever, Jaguar was so confident of its image that it did not trouble to add any badges on the tail.

pressings, most of them sourced from outside suppliers. Jaguar's own body production lines then welded up a three-dimensional jigsaw and where joints did not match perfectly, pounds and pounds of lead were melted, run into place and smoothed out with files and hammers. By modern standards, with more now known about lead fumes, this seems highly reprehensible, but such things were accepted in those days, and no one seemed to complain.

A drop-head coupé version of this new style followed later – first deliveries did not take place until the autumn of 1949, a full year after – and although it followed the same basic lines the coupé was structurally different. Not only was it a two-door shell (once again, the doors were hinged at the rear), but there was a great deal more wood in the make-up of the bodyshell. Like the old 'Mk IV' model, the fold-back top was fully trimmed and padded, with a 'De Ville' position allowing fresh air over the front seats only, and with external 'landau bars' supporting the fold-down linkage.

Jaguar's much-airbrushed impression of the Mk V drop-head coupé, as launched in 1948. The chassis and running gear, of course, was shared with that of the Mk V saloon, but from the screen back the shell itself was entirely special.

The Mk V's facia was as fully stocked with instruments as any enthusiast could wish. The rev counter's warning sector starts at 4,500rpm.

Although conceived in Britain's gloomiest post-war austerity period, there was no lack of luxury inside the new Mk V. As everyone had come to expect, the seats were leather faced, the facia panel was based on polished wood and there were good-quality carpets on the floor. The heater/de-mister was standard (this was still by no means usual in British cars, even at this price level), and a Radiomobile radio was optional.

As usual the large 18in (45cm) diameter steering wheel was rather handsome, though the overall control layout was rather spoiled by the use of an 'umbrella handle' handbrake which was tucked away under the steering column.

Blood relative! The sensational XK120 sports car, launched in 1948, used a shortened version of the new Mk V's chassis frame, the same suspensions, steering and transmission, but used the brand-new twin-cam XK engine.

OVERSHADOWED BY THE XK120

The Mk V made its debut at London's Earls Court Motor Show in October 1948. Since this was the first post-war British motor show, the Mk V might have been expected to cause a stir – except for one thing. Like every other car there, the Mk V was completely overshadowed by the new XK120!

Somehow, though, the XK120 was still seen as a dream car, rather than as something which would be immediately available. Jaguar-watchers could always see that the Mk V was commercially vital. But in October 1948 none of them realized that the Mk V was not yet ready to go on sale, for tooling had not yet been completed. Orders, particularly export orders, built up rapidly, but could not be satisfied until 1949 and later. 'Mk IV' assembly continued until March 1949, when the lines were finally cleared, and Mk V assembly took over.

Naturally the Mk V got a warm reception from the British motoring media. Looking back nearly half a century, it is easy to see how much British motoring writers were still afflicted by the 'British-is-Best' disease; they always praised new models and seemed prepared to believe everything that was claimed for a new car. Jaguar's own display advertising claimed that:

> ... the new Saloon is a brilliant successor to a long line of distinguished forerunners ... The new Jaguar is a better Jaguar, a finer-looking Jaguar, but is still unmistakably a Jaguar, and more than ever the finest car of its class in the world.

'Twenty important new features' were claimed for the Mk V saloon and nineteen for the drop-head coupé, some as important as the use of independent front suspension and some as minor as 'ventilation in the rear compartment'.

The Autocar thought that 'The new Mk V shows a very obvious improvement in appearance ...', while *The Motor* commented that '... the body has been completely restyled and now possesses an entirely new elegance ... an appearance which brings it up to date without in any way offending its many admirers'.

Although the car was still not ready to go on sale, the new Mk V was given the following UK prices (including tax) when previewed in October 1948: saloon and drop-head coupé (2½-litre), £1,189; saloon and drop-head coupé (3½-litre), £1,263. More importantly, with the British taxation regime in mind, the basic price of all these cars was comfortably under the £1,000 mark. Above that line, much higher rates of Purchase Tax were being levied.

Incidentally, although the drop-head coupé must surely have cost more to produce than the saloon, Jaguar had set the same price to stimulate demand. As statistics now show, that strategy failed.

It is also interesting to compare these with the prices some of Jaguar's rivals were asking for their own high-performance cars: Bentley Mk VI, £4,038; Bristol 400, £2,724; Daimler DB18, £1,977; Lagonda 2½-litre, £3,109; Riley 2½-litre, £1,125. With the single exception of Riley, no other manufacturer could come close to matching Jaguar's offering of performance and style. Then, as for many years afterwards, Jaguar offered what seemed to be unbeatable value for money.

A TWO-YEAR CAREER

Although almost everyone connected with Jaguar – management, dealers, customers and enthusiasts alike – all seemed to realize that the Mk V was strictly an interim model, this never harmed its reputation. In a production life of a mere twenty-eight months, no fewer than 10,466 cars were

Jaguar Mk V – 3 ½-litre and 2 ½-litre (1949–51)

[Full specification shown for 3½-litre; 2½-litre figures are given in brackets.]

Numbers built
10,466

Layout
Box-section chassis frame with separate steel bodyshell. Five-seater, front engine/rear drive, sold as four-door saloon, or drop-head coupé.

Engine
Type	Jaguar (previously SS-Jaguar) ohv
Block material	Cast iron
Head material	Cast iron
Cylinders	6 in-line
Cooling	Water
Bore and stroke	82 x 110mm (73 x 106mm)
Capacity	3,485cc (2,664cc)
Main bearings	7
Valves	2 per cylinder, pushrod and rocker operation
Compression ratio	6.75:1 (7.3:1)
Carburettors	2 SU 1.5in (2 SU 1.375in)
Max. power	125bhp @ 4,250rpm (102bhp @ 4,600rpm)

Transmission
Four-speed manual gearbox, with synchromesh on top, third and second gears.

Clutch	Single dry plate; hydraulically operated

Internal gearbox ratios
Top	1.00
3rd	1.34
2nd	1.94
1st	3.37
Reverse	3.37
Final drive	4.3:1 or 4.27:1 (4.55:1)

Suspension and steering
Front	Independent, torsion bars, wishbones, anti-roll bar, telescopic dampers
Rear	Live (beam) axle, by half-elliptic leaf springs, hydraulic lever-arm dampers
Steering	Recirculating ball
Tyres	6.70-16in cross-ply

Wheels	Steel disc, bolt-on
Rim width	5in
Brakes	
Type	Drum brakes at front and rear, hydraulically operated
Size	12in diameter drums
Dimensions (in/mm)	
Track	
Front	56/1,422
Rear	57.5/1,460
Wheelbase	120/3,048
Overall length	187/4,750
Overall width	68.5/1,740
Overall height	62.5/1,587
Unladen weight	3,696lb/1,676kg (Drop-head 3,808lb/1,727kg)

sold. Once assembly had got into its stride, more than a hundred Mk Vs were completed at Foleshill every week.

In all that time, few major technical changes were made, though a lot of chassis up-dating connected with the forthcoming Mk VII design was carried out. As with most other British cars of the period, far more cars were ordered in Britain than could ever be supplied, for UK sales were always restricted to give preference to overseas deliveries.

Jaguar was so confident of its ability to sell every Mk V that could be built, that there was no rush to supply test cars to *The Autocar* and *The Motor*. In fact the 2½-litre version was never submitted to test.

The Autocar borrowed a 3½-litre saloon, HVC 837, for test in July 1949 and dutifully gushed over it. Recording a top speed of 91mph (146km/h), with 0–60mph in 18.9 seconds, along with: 'the smooth surge of power which accelerates the car with supreme ease', the testers thought that this made 'an already fine car still more satisfying'. However, performance standards have certainly moved on, for in the 1990s the Mk V, at full stretch, could easily be seen off by almost every small family car on the road, especially on twisty roads.

Of the chassis the team wrote that:

The new suspension shows great merit both in comfort of riding for all occupants and in the stability for fast cornering. The long torsion bars in front ... gave a ride which is soft but never sloppy, and the car feels under remarkably good control. Up to the highest speeds it sits down on the road like a train, feeling completely safe.

The highest praise can be given to the Burman recirculating ball type of steering now fitted ... The steering ratio is low.

Predictably, there was also this comment:

For its remarkable combination of virtues it might well be expected in these days to cost several hundred pounds more than it does, and that is a very big tribute to be able to pay a car. Only in the high-quality British car of which this is a top-rank representative are performance, comfort and safety, with the accent on safety, so admirably blended'.

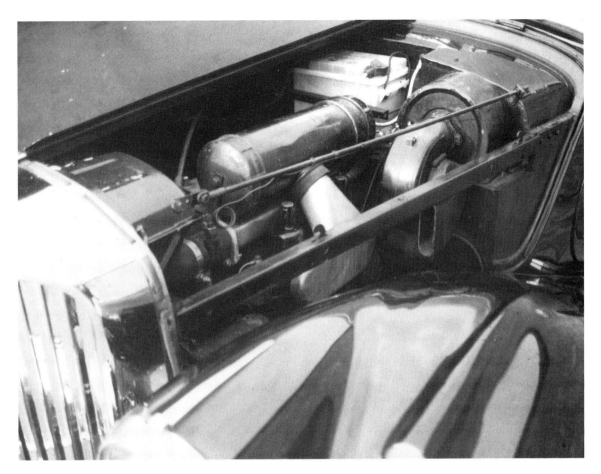

In the Mk V, the big 3½-litre pushrod engine was tucked well down into the engine bay. On the inlet (left) side of the unit, access was further hindered by the presence of the heater assembly.

Nine months later *The Motor* tried a different car, keeping it for 2,600 miles. For some reason the magazine carefully obliterated the registration number from photographs published in the test itself (probably because that was a different car!), but later it was seen to be JRW 660. Although the recorded top speed was almost identical to *The Autocar's* example – 90.8mph – acceleration was significantly faster, with 0–60mph being achieved in 14.7 seconds.

(To the author's knowledge, incidentally, this difference was quite usual for that period, where *The Autocar* used a fifth-wheel and calibrated speedometer, while *The Motor* merely recalibrated the vehicle's own speedometer, not always totally accurately.)

The end-of-test summary told its own story:

Judged simply on its merits as a powerful car of high quality, the Mk V Jaguar earns extremely high marks. When the relatively small price gap between it and other cars of very much more mundane character is taken into consideration, it becomes evident

It is not merely the overall style, but the detail of a Jaguar like the Mk V which tells us how careful William Lyons was with the shaping of his cars. There is nothing out of place here and you have to look extremely hard even to find evidence of door handles and turn indicators.

that the combination of performance, refinement and stamina which it offers is altogether outstanding.

By this time the Mk V was already beyond the half-way point of its career and needed no further boost to demand. The Mk VII, complete with its twin-cam XK engine, was nearly ready to be launched in October 1950, and to make way for space in the machine shops there had been some rationalization.

Manufacture of 2½-litre engines for the Mk V actually ended in the summer of 1950, and deliveries of 2½-litre-engined Mk Vs had virtually ceased before the Mk VII appeared. Even so, in spite of the big demand for the cars (and substantial evidence that buyers

were ready to pay a premium – unofficially – to get to the front of the queues!) Mk V prices had never been increased.

For these reasons, in that two-year period the breakdown of home-versus-export sales, and of model types, is significant:

Model	UK Deliveries	Export Deliveries	Total
2½-litre saloon	1,114	533	1,647
3½-litre saloon	3,124	4,690	7,814
2½-litre drop-head	1	27	28
3½-litre drop-head	137	840	977
Totals	4,376	6,090	10,466

The 2½-litre drop-head model had a particularly short career – January to May 1950 – which explains the tiny production figures. Although seventeen of the cars had right-hand-steering, only one such car was sold in the UK. The 3½-litre models were always more popular than 2½-litre models, which must have pleased Lyons, who charged £74 more for a car which cost no more to produce!

Even though the new Mk VII went into production at the end of 1950, the Mk V was not withdrawn at once. For a time almost every Mk VII was exported so the last batch of Mk Vs held the line in British Jaguar showrooms. The last Mk V of all was produced in June 1951, seven months after the Mk VII had gone on sale.

The distinguished Jaguar authority, Paul Skilleter, described the Mk V thus:

> Despite its traditional styling, the Mk V Jaguar was really the first subtle Jaguar; journey times were no longer simply a function of sheer engine power, but of a scientifically designed chassis too ….

In addition there was the impression of the Mk V's style. At once bulkier but no less sleek than the 'Mk IV', these were thoroughly practical high-performance machines. With more space, more practicality, but no less pace than the first-generation Jaguars, they were deservedly popular. In fact, an exceptional design would be needed to improve on the Mk V – and in 1950 the Mk VII was to become that car.

4 Mk VII: Grace, Space and Pace

As already explained in the previous chapter, the car we know as the Mk VII appeared later than Jaguar would have wished, which meant that the Mk V had to act as an (albeit very successful) interim model for more than two years. On the other hand, there's no doubt that the enforced delay was worthwhile, for the new XK engine was all the better for two more years' evolution.

As always in those more 'innocent' days, few Jaguar enthusiasts knew what sort of new saloon car was coming before they saw the new model described in the world's press. All they knew – or hoped that they knew – was that the fabulous new XK engine would find a home in the modern Mk V-type chassis.

Accordingly, it is no exaggeration to suggest that the arrival of the Mk VII caused a

Although built on the same basic chassis as the Mk V, the Mk VII of 1950 seemed to be a much larger car. Certainly it had a roomier cabin and the style was totally fresh.

Why no Mk VI?

When Jaguar came to replace the Mk V model in 1950, it named its new saloon the Mk VII. Then, and later, there was lively interest in the jump from 'V' to 'VII'. Had there been a secret Mk VI project, subsequently abandoned, or were there simpler reasons for this?

The solution, it seems, was to be found at Crewe, in the Rolls-Royce factory, where a car known as the Bentley Mk VI was produced from 1946 to 1952. When William Lyons came to name his new model in 1950, he did not want to confuse anyone by using the same nomenclature as an existing, and highly successful, Bentley. (The fact that a Bentley Mk V had briefly gone on sale in 1939/40 did not seem to deter him when naming the Jaguar Mk V though!)

Although early XK engines were tested in Jaguar Mk Vs, before Mk VII bodyshells became available, there was never any intention to sell cars of that type – which lays to rest the seductive theory of such a mechanically interesting 'Mk VI' being a half-way house between the two types.

As 'Lofty' England later recalled:

There was never any idea of fitting the XK engine on a production basis – in fact, that engine was not set up for production when the Mk V was introduced. To prove the Mk V's handling, ride and so on, the experimental department fitted two cars with XK engines; one was an existing Mk V, the other a new car built as a 'Mk VI' for Sir William.

Sir William sold that car to George Hack, an old motorcycle friend ....

Incidentally, when Bentley came to update its own Mk VI, Jaguar's Mk VII had gone on sale, so a new name – R-Type – had to be chosen for the new Bentley. The biter bit!

sensation. At first sight, the Mk VII was startling in so many ways – astonishingly fast with a technically advanced engine, all wrapped in a smooth new shape and listed at a quite remarkable price.

Not only was this a remarkably graceful machine for such a large design, but it was also the very first Jaguar to use a complete bodyshell supplied by an outside supplier: the Pressed Steel Co. Ltd of Cowley, near Oxford. At an early stage in the planning for this new machine, Lyons had concluded that Pressed Steel could provide more bodyshells than his cramped workshops could produce and at the right price.

First impressions, of course, were that this was not only a very fast, but also a very large car. Even though the Mk VII rode on the same wheelbase – the same basic chassis, even – as the Mk V, it looked bulkier, and by definition, heavier than its elegant old predecessor. Even though William Lyons was wholly dedicated to producing the best possible shape for all his cars, because of the full-width style of the Mk VII this was almost inevitable.

There was also one truly vital marketing difference between the Mk V and Mk VII models. In many ways the Mk V had looked traditional, with a style which appealed to old-style 'British Empire' markets. The Mk VII, on the other hand, was aimed fair and square at the most exciting export market of all – North America.

SHAPING THE MK VII

It is now fairly clear that for the Mk VII Lyons had taken a great deal of time to get a shape with which he was satisfied, especially as he always had to consider the demands that Pressed Steel's production engineers would later make. As we now know, although he had taken very little time – and with no discarded themes – to evolve the shape of the

XK120, that process could not immediately be repeated with the Mk VII project.

For the XK120, in 1948, Lyons had made the big styling leap – from shaping cars to have flowing, separate wings and running boards, to cars which were full-width machines, with more sweeping lines and, hopefully, with integrated nose and front wing shapes.

It is now generally agreed that the shape of the original XK120 was inspired by the special BMW 328 built to take part in the 1940 Mille Miglia and subsequently brought into the UK by AFN in 1947, though there were other pointers – specials and one-off bodies – which he might also have seen, and noted, along the way.

Built on a much-shortened Mk V chassis, though fitted with the all-new XK engine, the XK120 was an overnight success. It was that very success which caused further delay to the Mk VII programme, as Lyons's decision to have the XK120 bodyshell properly re-tooled, with panels to be supplied by the Pressed Steel Co. Ltd, meant further demands on his own staff and on Pressed Steel itself.

Since the use of the 120in (3,048mm) wheelbase Mk V-style chassis frame had already been decided, there was no delay in settling on the new car's platform. Except for using a slighter wider rear axle (to ensure even more space in the cabin), even the suspension and all of its details were the same as before.

It seems to have been at this point that William Lyons the artist took over from William Lyons the businessman. Having agreed with his engineering chief, Bill Heynes, on the basic layout of the chassis (the fore-and-aft position of the bulky engine would govern the position of the bulkhead, the cooling radiator and the location of engine bay panels, for instance), he could begin to shape his first truly post-war saloon. Incidentally, it seems that the drop-head

coupé alternative was barely explored – if only because to produce this as an alternative to the Pressed Steel-built saloon would have been too costly and difficult.

Consider, now, how you or I might have started out on this process. We would probably have used the Mk V chassis, but brought the body style up to date by widening the body, pushing out the sides, smoothing out the nose, and using the same sort of side profile as the new XK120. Easy … In fact, we would probably have made a real hash of it and the initial result would have looked awful.

In fact the Mk VII shape did not develop in one phase, but in a whole series of 'look-see' efforts, all of which had to be investigated. For Lyons, the styling of a new car was not something to be rushed. As far as is known, he never worked on scale models, but always oversaw the development of full-size mock-ups. Having settled on the basic architecture of the machine, he would get Fred Gardner's tiny development shop to start building up a shell, using a boxy skeleton of wooden sections (the profile of which could easily and quickly be modified), to which shaped steel panels were then fixed. Invariably, at this stage, they were painted black. Then, using no more than his own instincts and verbal instructions to Gardner's team, he would mastermind the production of a complete mock-up. Somehow, in spite of his extremely busy life, he found time to visit this department every day.

As a young designer at Jaguar, with a drawing board close to windows looking out on the outside world, I would often see that unmistakable white-haired figure striding across the road from the main office block into the main factory block in Brown's Lane. Although he was on his way to a dusty workshop – and would very probably divert to peer into some detail of the assembly lines along the way – he was always immaculately dressed, usually in a blue suit. (Out of office

The shape established by William Lyons in 1948, for introduction as the Mk VII of 1950, was still acceptable ten years later. This car, in fact, is a late-1950s Mk VIII, complete with duotone colour scheme.

The basic chassis frame design established with the Mk V model was used under all 'Big Jaguars' built up until 1961. This photograph was taken in 1957, and shows the sturdy nature of that frame.

hours, Sir William was sometimes seen in casual dress, but he was never scruffy.) What usually followed is best summed up by comments made in the 1950s by one of *Autocar's* most percipient writers, Michael Brown:

> At Jaguar's they tend to smile at the idea of studio settings for elegant young men as aids to artistic interpretation (though a geranium or two is not despised on the drawing office window sill). Jaguar styling is three-dimensional, sculptural.
>
> A mock-up is made and altered until it is right, Sir William pacing round it, accentuating a curve here, straightening a line there, until it is right from every angle.

Such a man, you might think, would paint in oils or landscape his garden. But if the more orthodox creativeness is there – and there can be no doubt that it is – car manufacture has not spared the time for it to develop. Yet it would be strange indeed if it did not result in some classically artistic achievement; in gaining the Jaguar car the world may have lost a great sculptor.

Except for the XK120, his first efforts were rarely successful, but since the wooden construction of mock-ups was cheap and cheerful there was little delay or expense involved in scrapping a buck and starting again. Lyons's view was that it was better to take

It took a long time to settle the style for the Mk VII. Here, circa 1948, is a mock-up which has been hauled out into the open air for Lyons to inspect. The 'dirty white sheet background' was traditional in those days! The wing line of this example owes a lot to the XK120.

With the Mk VII, Jaguar finally produced a style with totally enclosed headlamps. Even then, the company was at pains to make the headlamps that important bit different in detail – note the 'J' decal in the centre of the glass.

time and get it right, than to rush something out to the public.

From time to time – always at weekends and always well shielded from public gaze – the mock-up would be lifted out of the workshop and placed in the middle of a car park or field, where Lyons (and sometimes one or two of his favoured lieutenants) would walk round it, viewing it from a distance. Not only was this done to get a better all-round perspective, but to see how the light affected the various shapes, curves and angles. Glossy black paint ensured that nothing was missed.

Photographs in Jaguar's archive confirm that the development of the Mk VII shape was a long and painful process, and that Lyons was clearly noting every styling cue

By 1949 the future Mk VII style was almost settled. As is obvious from the shot, sheet metal panels were fixed to a wooden skeleton. Although the wing line is finalized, the contour of the side window cut-out is still not quite settled.

Although the Mk VII's bodyshell was totally new, it was obviously a development of previous Jaguar shapes, as this tail aspect proves. Like later Jaguar saloons, it featured twin fuel tank filler cap covers and the usual sausage-style rear window shape.

Mk VII / Mk VIII styling details – not just neat handles to help lift the boot lid, but lockable handles as well, which swivelled when released.

used by his rivals. Widening the main cabin to eliminate running boards was relatively straightforward, but settling on a graceful nose was not.

The very first efforts featured a nose rather like that of the existing Lagonda 2½-litre, while an Alfa Romeo 1900-type nose with a high and narrow grille was also tried. Shells were mocked up with V-screens or with single-piece glass, headlamps were high or low, wide or closely set, small or large, while grilles expanded or contracted to suit changes in the theme.

Most importantly, the shape of the flanks – in particular the method of linking up the shape of the front wings with the rear – went through as much modification. XK120-like styles were tried, but were not liked. A 'straight-through' style almost uncannily like that which would be adopted for the monocoque 2.4 five years later was also assessed and finally the familiar shape which is now known so well was chosen.

After a great deal of detail work had been completed – headlamp positions, foglamps to suit, bumpers, chrome, door handle shapes and function – Jaguar was finally able to call in Pressed Steel and commission the body tooling. Then there was a long wait because Pressed Steel was really frantically busy at this time. Fortunately the Cowley-based business had already created the first series of new post-war bodies for Austin, Morris, Wolseley, Rootes, Rover and Rolls-Royce by this time, but it still took ages for them to prepare press tools for every new panel.

Not only did the Mk VII look very different from the Mk V, but there were major differences in construction. For the first time on a saloon, for instance, Jaguar used a one-piece bonnet panel, which was hinged at the scuttle and gave much improved access to the engine bay. Both front and rear doors were now hinged at the front. Not only was the luggage boot intrinsically larger than before, but because the spare wheel was positioned

at the side it could also be a lot deeper and much more capacious.

JAGUAR'S FIRST TWIN-CAM ENGINED SALOON

Now that twin-ohc with four valves per cylinder and sophisticated fuel injection appear in many family hatchbacks these days, we all tend to be very blasé about them, so it's easy to discount the importance of Jaguar's new XK engine when it appeared in the late 1940s. With its long stroke and its massive architecture, maybe it already looks archaic today – but at the time it represented a huge leap forward.

Quite simply, the XK engine was the world's first quantity-production twin-cam unit. Previous twin-cams had either been racing units or had been derived from them. All were very costly to build and finicky to keep in tune. Before the XK engine was unveiled, the only twin-cams to go on sale in small numbers had been fitted to opulent machines, like the American Duesenbergs, or to tiny numbers of Alfa Romeos built with little regard to profitability, only to company (and national) image.

The mass-production cars of the late 1940s usually had simple overhead-valve engines, though European Fords, some Morris and Rootes models and a number of American cars still used archaic side-valve designs, but none of them could even approach the specific power of the new XK unit. When they saw the XK engine for the first time (and subsequently accepted, however reluctantly, that it was indeed destined for production!) Jaguar's main rivals must have been appalled by the implications. Quite simply, they would eventually have to match it or be defeated along the way.

During those now-famous fire-watching sessions at the Foleshill factory, William Lyons's vision had been of a post-war Jaguar company which would sell more cars, more technically advanced cars, than before. To do this, he envisaged a new range, with new engines, all of which were to set new standards.

Right from the start he was insistent that the new saloon should have a top speed of at least 100mph (160km/h). Though this may sound tame by modern standards, in the 1940s it was truly ambitious. In 1945, for instance, there wasn't a series production car in Europe which could exceed 100mph (160km/h). In the 1930s market only a handful of production cars of any sort could reach 100mph and those which did were usually exotic sports cars, with hand-built chassis, sold at colossal prices. Owing to the dislocation caused by the war, little had changed in the decade which followed.

TRIM AND FURNISHING

We often forget that it is not engineering which usually sells cars in showrooms, but looks, style and furnishings. That was why the looks of the new Mk VII, and what was inside its large cabin, were going to be so important, especially when the first examples arrived in North America.

At first glance, the Mk VII appeared to be a much larger and more spacious car than

A subtle 'Jaguar' badge on the wheel covers was all that was needed to remind people of the make involved.

the Mk V which it had replaced. Not only was the body width ostensibly greater than before, but the XK engine was mounted further forward in the frame, which ought to have allowed the front passenger bulkhead to creep forward after it, which in turn should have been translated into extra space in the cabin.

To assess whether this was indeed the case, it is useful to study the dimensional drawings which were published in magazine road tests, where the plan views are most instructive. Not only was the front end of the Mk VII bodyshell considerably wider than that of the Mk V, but, owing to the general

shape of the cabin, so also was the middle of the body. Naturally there was extra lounging room in the rear, but in fact it was the front seat passengers – and especially the driver – who were going to benefit the most. For a start, the seats of the Mk VII were considerably wider than before: 24.5in (62cm) compared with 20in (51cm). That was the good news, the bad news was that they had far less shaping and could not be expected to hold the passengers' bodies in place under hard cornering. Neither, for that matter, were they height-adjustable.

Across the front seats of the car, however, at shoulder height where the driver needed

By comparison with the rest of the interior decoration, Mk VII/VIII door trim panels were simply laid out.

elbow space, the Mk VII was considerably wider: 59in (150cm) instead of 51in (130cm). There was a couple of extra inches headroom above the seats and the front footwell space was much as before.

The increase in rear-seat space was also very obvious. The old Mk V had measured 54in (137cm) across the rear seats at its widest point, whereas the equivalent Mk VII dimension was 59in (150cm). Headroom had been increased by 3in (7.5cm), and the total leg room (cushion length plus leg space) was also larger by 3.5in (9cm). All this was complemented by a new rear seat position well ahead of the line of the rear axle (the squab of the Mk V had been above that line) and by a much larger stowage boot.

Perhaps the Mk VII was still not quite as spacious as the latest domestic North American models, but there was certainly nothing for which Jaguar salesmen would have to apologize. Here, in fact, was the first (probably the only for many years) British car which would properly appeal to American buyers used to acres of space in their own domestic products.

It might be that the latest in Cadillacs, Lincolns and Oldsmobiles had even more

A simple tool kit fitted into the dropdown panel normally folded away into a front door trim panel.

The Mk VII's instrument panel was laid out on traditional Jaguar lines, complete with pillar-to-pillar wood veneer and the contra-rotating rev-counter and speedometer needles.

space inside – particularly in the front where there was usually a bench seat clad in shiny imitation leather – but there were no American cars offering the same grace and British club-land image. In particular, no American car-maker could match the British genius in combining real wood, real leather and real carpets, together with the indefinable aromas and atmosphere which went with them.

XK – THE NEW TWIN-CAM ENGINE

Initially, when the XK engine made its debut in 1948, few believed that Jaguar really

intended to put it into quantity production. Quite simply, there were no precedents – neither in the UK, nor in the rest of the world.

Yet by 1950 Jaguar's fabulous new power unit had already made its name. Originally intended for launch in the Mk VII saloon,

Footnote: In 1950, for sure, the Mk VII was the most powerful car on the British market, its 160bhp rating being exactly matched by that of the current Cadillac. Although there was a 180bhp Chrysler in that year, I know of no other production-car engine which could match it.

The birth of the XK engine

Jaguar's famous XK engine, which powered every six-cylinder Jaguar built from 1951 to 1983, was conceived during wartime fire-watching sessions on Sunday night at the Foleshill factory from 1943 to 1945. It was unveiled in 1948 as the XK120's power unit, and was the only Jaguar passenger-car engine produced from 1950 to 1971. Although a new 'six' – the AJ6 design – was introduced in 1983, the old-type XK engine was still produced until the early 1990s, not only for spares, but to power the long-running Daimler limousine, a descendant of the Mk X/420G.

William Lyons wanted his post-war engines to be powerful; to look powerful, but also to be smooth, refined and reliable. This was a difficult, but not impossible, brief for William Heynes, Claude Baily and Walter Hassan to meet, but history proves that they achieved the standard.

The first projects encompassed a family of four-cylinder and six-cylinder engines. The very first prototype was a twin-cam four-cylinder XF unit, while the second was the BMW-style cross-pushrod XG, which was actually a conversion of a Standard Flying Fourteen/Jaguar 1.5-litre unit.

The true forerunner was the XJ, in which the four-cylinder version had bore and stroke dimensions of 80.5 x 98mm (a capacity of 1,996cc), the six an 83mm bore, a 98mm stroke and 3,182cc. Before the new design was revealed, this matured as the XK, where the stroke of the six-cylinder engine was lengthened to 106mm, to provide more power-speed torque – the definitive 3,442cc engine was therefore born.

Production, on a limited scale, began in 1949 for the XK120, at which point the XK unit was the world's only twin-ohc in series production. In the next two decades the six-cylinder XK engine was used in all the famous Jaguar models, being produced in 2,483cc, 3,442cc, 3,781cc and eventually 4,235cc form. The four-cylinder engine, though shown to the public in 1948, was never put into production.

Not only did the XK engine power every large Jaguar saloon from the Mk VII to the 420G, but it also powered machines as diverse as the E-Type sports cars, the XJ6 range, the famous C-Type and D-Type racing Jaguars, and the Alvis Scorpion armoured military vehicle. It was, and still is, a legend in its own lifetime, and has been fitted to hundreds of thousands of magnificent Jaguars.

and with production tooling organized on that basis, it had first been pressed into service in the XK120 sports car. The numbers involved were limited at first and the schedule quite relaxed, which meant that almost every teething problem except that of heavy oil consumption had been eliminated before the Mk VII finally appeared.

The concept, birth and development of the famous twin-cam XK engine is now so well documented that few details need to be repeated here. It is enough, surely, to note that in its original tune, where it developed 160bhp (gross) at 5,200rpm, it was already one of the most powerful production engines in the world.

With its twin-ohc valve gear, its aluminium cylinder head and its carefully crafted details, not only was it a magnificently engineered engine, but it also looked impressive too. If there was anything more likely to impress a neighbour than the noise of an XK engine, it was the view of its polished camshaft and chaincase covers when the bonnet was raised. And yet, as every Mk VII owner soon discovered, it was not only powerful, but completely docile. Because its cylinder head breathed so well and because it had such a sturdy bottom-end construction, the combination of a lengthy cylinder stroke and relatively 'touring' cam profiles meant that it could pull lustily from very low engine revs.

Immediately after Ron 'Soapy' Sutton had demonstrated that the XK120 could beat 130mph (210km/h) on Belgium's Jabbeke highway in 1949, he returned and trickled past a group of motoring journalists at a mere 5mph (8km/h) in top gear! This, mark you, was with a car prepared for speed work and fitted with an ultra-high (non-standard) final drive ratio, so the same sort of flexibility could be guaranteed in a Mk VII saloon.

In the Mk VII the XK engine was in precisely the same tune as that fitted to the XK120, at least according to the catalogue, that is. Under the bonnet the only discernible difference was that Mk VIIs were fitted with a large circular section carburettor air cleaner, while there was no space for this fitment in an XK120.

The air cleaner must have stifled a little of the XK engine's top-end power, but Jaguar never admitted to this. In any case, the 160bhp was a 'gross' (test-bed) figure. Since I personally witnessed Bill Heynes 'designing' power curves for publication on a complaisant designer's drawing board (so that they looked good, rather than were totally accurate), I do not propose to argue about detail.

The way to check up on an XK engine's flexibility is to witness the low-speed pulling power of such a car. Another way is to study the top-gear acceleration figures published in road tests. When *The Autocar* tested its first Mk VII in 1952, these top-gear figures tell their own story:

10–30mph (15–50km/h), 8.1 seconds;
30–50mph (50–80km/h), 8.3 seconds;
50–70mph (80–110km/h), 10.7 seconds.

All of which proves that the torque curve must have been as lusty low down as it was in the middle-range.

The XK engine, frankly, was so remarkable that it would have made a very ordinary car totally acceptable in its own right. Fortunately for Jaguar, the rest of the Mk VII (and XK120) model was up to the same high standard.

MK VII RUNNING GEAR

Too many people assume that the Mk VII simply 'picked up' the Mk V chassis, into which a new-fangled XK engine had been inserted. This was not true. Although it was based on that of the Mk V, the Mk VII's chassis and running gear was different in many detailed ways.

Although the XK engine itself was obviously new and the chassis frame itself was virtually identical, it supported a modified front suspension, different servo-assisted brakes, a widened rear axle, and a repositioned front anti-roll bar.

To gain a lot more space in the cabin, the engine/gearbox assembly was pushed forward by 5in (12cm), and since the XK engine was itself longer than the venerable 3½-litre pushrod overhead-valve unit this meant that the cooling radiator had to be no less than 8in (20cm) nearer the nose than it had been in the Mk V. This, of course, was a very good reason why the front end style of the Mk VII had to look the way it did.

The gearbox was as previously used in the Mk V, as was the Salisbury rear axle except that the track was slightly widened. Owing to the extra bulk of the XK engine, the front suspension and steering layout had to be altered, one obvious move being the relocation of the front anti-roll bar.

The braking system, too, was changed, the Girling drums getting a trailing shoe arrangement at the front, and a vacuum servo to provide assistance. This servo, mounted on the chassis frame near the cruciform section, looked vulnerable but worked surprisingly well in practice.

Unhappily the steering gear was still low geared, and became even more low-geared when a different steering box was standardized early in the production run. This was done, of course, to keep steering effort down, for power assistance was not yet available in the British motor industry – it would not

There is seemingly more space in the Mk VII engine bay than in that of the obsolete Mk V, though the bad news was that the inner wheel arch panels were fixed in place and access to almost everything below cylinder head level involved a stretch for the mechanics.

Detail of the engine oil filler cap, complete with the delicate profiled 'Jaguar' badge.

even be available on Rolls-Royce models until 1956 (and then as an extra). In those days American cars, with which the Mk VII would have to compete, had even lower-geared steering.

MK VII ON THE MARKET

The new car was announced on the eve of the Earls Court Motor Show in October 1950, so it was altogether fitting that William Lyons, acting as President of the Society of Motor Manufacturers and Traders, should escort HRH Princess Margaret on her tour of the stands after she had officially opened the exhibition.

Lyons thought the first appearance of the Mk VII was so important that he chartered special trains to transport his entire workforce to and from London to see the Mk VII on display, at a venue where it almost immediately got the unofficial title of 'Car of the Show'. He must have been infuriated when his company then became involved in industrial strife, and the same workforce then went on strike.

Some good, however, often follows misfortune and in this case the six-week hiatus at the Foleshill factory allowed the

The graceful leaping Jaguar mascot featured on so many splendid Jaguars – later to be hounded out of existence by safety regulations.

Jaguar Cars Inc. (of the USA)

Without the sales achieved in North America, I doubt if Jaguar could ever have made any money from its sports cars, which might also have meant that it could not have produced such successful saloons. In the 25-year period covered by this book, nearly 100,000 cars were sold in that vast continent.

The first post-war Jaguars were 3½-litres, sent to the USA in 1947, when Max Hoffman began selling cars on the East Coast. Chuck Hornburg soon undertook a similar task on the West Coast. Then, in 1952, Johannes Eerdmans arrived in the USA, later to direct Jaguar's transatlantic sales until he retired in 1971.

Sir William Lyons had met Eerdmans during the war, and it was his recommendations which led to Hoffman relinquishing the Jaguar franchise. Jaguar Cars' North American Corporation was set up in 1954, this company later becoming Jaguar Cars Inc. in 1958.

Although the majority of North American sales went to the sports cars – XKs and later E-Types – the Big Jaguars always figured strongly in these achievements:

Deliveries to the USA and Canada – to 1970

Financial Year (ending)	USA	Canada
1946 (31 July)	–	–
1947	7	–
1948	245	–
1949	135	12
1950	826	224
1951	1,552	182
1952	3,243	96
1953	5,218	275
1954	1,834	204
1955	3,239	182
1956	3,871	346
1957	3,592	347
1958	4,607	510
1959	5,596	808
1960	4,934	523
1961	3,422	609
1962	5,716	445
1963	4,113	211
1964	4,037	222
1965	3,669	237
1966	5,418	351
1967	6,702	323
1968	4,429	382
1969 (30 September – 14 months)	6,833	418
1970 (30 September)	7,384	433

engineers and production specialists to sort out problems with the first bodyshells which Pressed Steel had delivered.

The Mk VII was certainly worth waiting for. Launched at what looked like the ridiculously low UK price of £988 (basic) or £1,276 with Purchase Tax added in, it seemed to offer magnificent value. For British customers the problem was that it was firmly advertised as being 'for export only' at first, the vast majority of early supplies being aimed at North America, where it was unveiled in New York's Waldorf-Astoria hotel in November.

Although the Mk VII would not be more freely available in the UK until 1952, it is worth comparing it with its British rivals when it appeared. Since this was such a powerful machine, no less than 196in (4,978mm) long, and weighing nearly 4,000lb (1,800kg), it was clearly more substantial than almost anything with which it could be compared.

Even so, nothing could match the Mk VII on performance, and on value there was little to touch it. Armstrong-Siddeley's Sapphire was still two years away from launch. Alvis's TA21 3-litre was old-fashioned, could only reach 90mph (145km/h), and cost £1,598. Humber's Super Snipe was slightly cheaper, but much slower, with inferior handling. Riley's 2½-litre was graceful, but old-fashioned with a cramped interior and could only reach 95mph (153km/h). Jaguar, in other words, was still on its way to 'annihilating' all the rivals who had so dreaded its potential in the late 1930s and 1940s.

Almost at once, Jaguar's proud slogan 'Grace, Space and Pace' was linked to the Mk VII and there was no doubt that almost everyone was mightily impressed by what they saw. Maybe it was coincidence, but Jaguar was delighted to be placed next to Rolls-Royce on the floor of the Earls Court Exhibition Hall. Unless they put down their money, however, few had a chance to see whether the claims of 100mph-plus top speeds were justified, as Jaguar saw no need to make road test cars available.

By the end of 1950, when Mk VII deliveries finally began, it was quite clear that Jaguar had a problem. It was not one of having to find places where the cars could be sold, but of building enough cars to fulfil orders already placed. On the basis of the New York showing alone, 500 retail orders were taken, and before long it was obvious that production would have to be boosted, if at all possible.

The records show that Jaguar exports to the USA and Canada rose from 1,050 in 1949/50 to no less than 3,339 in 1951/2, and that they burgeoned further to 5,493 in 1952/3. That last figure, incidentally, represented no less than 54 per cent of Jaguar's output.

Well before this point, however, Lyons had concluded that he would have to move his business away from Foleshill. Applications to build extra factory space on undeveloped land alongside the existing plant in Foleshill had been refused, so in the end he concluded a deal with the Government to take over a much larger, ex-Daimler 'shadow' factory at Browns Lane, Allesley.

The move to Browns Lane was not completed until 1952 and was a gradual, phased process, with a new administration block being erected almost at once. Mk VII assembly, which began at Foleshill in December 1950, was finally moved to Allesley in 1952, when production rates could finally be pushed up. Incidentally, because the Browns Lane plant had originally been a Government 'shadow' factory, the sale to Jaguar included a requirement for Jaguar to tool-up for production of the Rolls-Royce Meteor engine for tanks (this being an unsupercharged development of the famous Merlin aero engine). Such activity ran down before the end of the 1950s, which was a blessing to Jaguar, for by this time its machine shops were bursting with activity.

By the mid-1950s Allesley was already producing more than 200 cars every week (most of them Mk VIIs) and by the end of that decade the production rate would be doubled yet again. In the early 1960s, Mk VII assembly continued to expand, British deliveries finally built up and a well-publicized competition record (covered in more detail in Chapter 6) all helped to build the new car's reputation.

When *The Autocar's* Gordon Wilkins drove the 'works' Mk VII in the 1952 Monte Carlo rally and used other cars to recce the route, he completed a total of 6,000 miles (9600km), describing the new model as: 'one of the most impressive cars available in the world today'.

Official road tests, published in April 1952, confirmed a top speed of 102mph (164km/h), with 0–60mph (0–100km/h) in 13.4 seconds, and an overall fuel consumption of 19mpg (15l/100km), the last figure being acceptable in view of the car's great size and carrying capacity. Everyone seemed to like the slide-back sunshine roof, which

Jaguar Mk VII (1950–4)

Numbers built
20,908

Layout
Box-section chassis frame with separate steel bodyshell. Five-seater, front engine/rear drive, sold as four-door saloon

Engine
Type	Jaguar XK
Block material	Cast iron
Head material	Cast aluminium
Cylinders	6 in-line
Cooling	Water
Bore and stroke	83 x 106mm
Capacity	3,442cc
Main bearings	7
Valves	2 per cylinder, operated by twin ohc, and inverted bucket-type tappets
Compression ratio	8.0:1 (or optional 7.0:1)
Carburettors	2 SU 1.75in
Max. power	160bhp @ 5,200rpm (150bhp @ 5,200 on 7.0:1 CR)
Max. torque	195lb/ft @ 2,500rpm

Transmission
Four-speed manual gearbox, with synchromesh on top, third and second gears

Clutch	Single dry plate; hydraulically operated

Internal gearbox ratios
Top	1.00
3rd	1.365
2nd	1.98
1st	3.37
Reverse	3.37
Final drive	4.27:1

Overdrive (Laycock) became optional, on top gear only, from January 1954, when the final drive ratio became 4.55:1. Internal transmission ratio was:

Top (O/D)	0.778

Automatic transmission (Borg Warner) became optional from March 1953. Internal gearbox ratios were:

Direct	1.00
Intermediate	1.44
Low	2.31

Reverse	2.0
Maximum torque multiplication	2.15
Final drive ratio	4.27:1

Suspension and steering
Front	Independent, torsion bars, wishbones, anti-roll bar, telescopic dampers
Rear	Live (beam) axle, by half-elliptic leaf springs, hydraulic lever-arm dampers (telescopic dampers from mid-1953)
Steering	Recirculating ball
Tyres	6.70-16in cross-ply
Wheels	Steel disc, bolt-on
Rim width	5in (5.5in from mid-1952)

Brakes
Type	Drum brakes at front and rear, hydraulically operated
Size	12in diameter drums

Dimensions (in/mm)
Track	
Front	56/1,422 (56.5/1,435 from mid-1952)
Rear	57.5/1,460 (58/1,473 from mid-1952)
Wheelbase	120/3,048
Overall length	196.5/4,991
Overall width	73.5/1,867
Overall height	62/1,575
Unladen weight	3,864lb/1,752kg

was a fast-disappearing body fitment at that time. In closing, *The Autocar* testers summarized that:

Considered from any angle, the Mk VII Jaguar is an outstanding car. It has extremely good performance, is very comfortable to drive and to ride in, is very completely equipped, has a modern yet dignified appearance, and is very good value – indeed, it is in that respect phenomenal.

The Motor was no less enthusiastic:

In the opinion of the test team the Jaguar, judged upon a basis of value for money and all-round merit, is one of the best cars submitted for Road Test in the post-war years.

Even to those of us who have been dissecting 'classic' period road tests for some years, it is not always easy to read between the lines, as one had to do in those days. There is little doubt, however, that the low-geared steering was not liked, the gearbox synchromesh action was poor and that there was quite a lot of brake fade when the servo-assisted drums were used hard. It was also thought that there was too much body roll on corners.

None of this was news to Jaguar's engineers, of course, who would have liked to make several improvements if only William Lyons had let them. Lyons, however, wanted to squeeze a lot more life out of the Moss-type gearbox, which would not be finally replaced until 1964/5, while power-steering and disc brakes were still not properly developed.

Browns Lane

Although all SS cars, all SS-Jaguars and early post-war Jaguars were produced at the Foleshill factory, this was bursting at the seams by 1950, and William Lyons began to look around for more factory space in Coventry. At this time the city was going through something of an industrial upheaval, not only because wholesale rebuilding to repair Second World War bomb damage was under way, but also because several of the original aero-engine shadow factories were becoming redundant.

The Government's shadow factory scheme was launched in 1936, as a way of boosting the re-armament programme, and particularly to get the motor industry involved in setting up, running and managing new aero-engine factories. No sooner was the first wave of factories up and running, than the Government initiated phase two, the result being that Daimler built 'Shadow No. 2' in Browns Lane, Allesley, a few miles to the west of Coventry. This building began by manufacturing Bristol Hercules radial engines during the War, but by the early 1950s it was closed down, Daimler having no further use for it.

After a great deal of negotiation with Government officials, Lyons was able to buy (not lease, which was more normal at this period in Government history) the factory, began moving his assembly facilities into place during 1952, and completed the move by the end of that year. Once the move was completed, the Foleshill factory was sold off, and all links with the SS and SS-Jaguar days on that site were dissolved.

Browns Lane has been the home of Jaguar ever since then, though it has been modified, expanded, re-jigged and persistently modernized ever since. The purchase of the Daimler business and its factories in Radford, and the opening up of the technical centre at Whitley, Coventry, have not changed that.

Even as recently as 1991, the city council opened a new road linking the Allesley bypass to Brownshill Green, in which a major feature was a new roundabout, and direct access to the old 'back gate', now the official 'new' main entrance to Browns Lane. Ford, which controlled Jaguar after 1989, also laid plans to invest in Browns Lane to produce ever more cars in the late 1990s and 2000s.

DEVELOPMENT CHANGES

The original Mk VII stayed in production for four years – specifically, from December 1950 to September 1954 – before being supplanted by the Mk VIIM, but many detail changes and improvements were made during that time.

Some changes, like the more rugged front suspension details, the stiffer damper settings and engine changes intended to cut down on oil leaks, were accompanied by the use of wider-rim road wheels, optional higher-lift camshafts and a modified gearbox. Telescopic dampers replaced lever-arm dampers at the rear in mid-1953.

Before the end of the run, Jaguar had also made a whole series of engine options available, the most extreme producing something akin to C-Type engine performance (and a claimed 210bhp); it was in this guise that Mk VIIs performed so startlingly well in British saloon car racing.

There were two major improvements to the transmission, for both Laycock de Normanville overdrive and Borg Warner automatic transmission became optional extras. As far as the American market was concerned, however, the major improvement was the addition of automatic transmission, this dating from March 1953, while the overdrive option (which operated only on top gear) was phased in from January 1954.

Captain de Normanville's overdrive had been under development for some years before Laycock took up the manufacturing rights. Several British manufacturers began testing the new unit – always fitted to the rear of an existing gearbox – in the late 1940s and while Standard-Triumph was the first to take the plunge, Jaguar was not far behind.

The secret was that this could truly be a clutchless gearchange, for operation of a cone clutch was by electrically-operated solenoid. At first this change could be rather lumpy, but persistent development helped to provide a change which was whisper-smooth in the 'change-up' direction, though down-changes of the over-run could be abrupt even on 1970s cars which used developments of this layout.

Some years before it adopted the Borg Warner Type DG automatic transmission (which was originally built in the USA, where Borg Warner was a major player in the automotive transmissions industry), Jaguar realized that it needed to use such a gearbox to satisfy a large number of North American buyers who were not used to anything else.

Like Rolls-Royce before them, Jaguar tried several different proprietary gearboxes (one of which, the GM Hydramatic, was eventually taken up by Rolls-Royce) before settling on the Borg Warner design. By current standards this was a conventional piece of kit, with three forward speeds, matched to a torque converter that allowed quite a lot of slip at lower engine speeds, which did nothing for the acceleration or the fuel consumption.

As other authorities have pointed out, the DG was by no means a sophisticated installation, but it was reliable, already proven and available 'off-the-shelf'. Once on offer, a growing number of Mk VIIs and their later developments were ordered with it. Jaguar, meantime, was preparing itself for even greater change in the mid-1950s. Not only had the C-Type and D-Type racing sports cars been developed, but a new compact car, the monocoque 2.4 saloon was also on the way. Somehow, though, the small Jaguar design team found time to make further improvements to the Mk VII, the result being the Mk VIIM.

5 Mks VIIM, VIII and IX

INTRODUCING THE MK VIIM

Four years after the Mk VII had been launched, its design was still developing steadily and no one expected it to be displaced. In any case, Jaguar could spare neither capital, design nor development time to produce an all-new model. When Jaguar therefore decided to freshen up its range in the autumn of 1954, there was no new saloon model, but simply an improved version – the Mk VIIM.

'M' for what? Jaguar never explained, but my best guess is that it stood for 'Modified'. In what we would now call a logical 'product planning' manoeuvre, the same basic mechanical changes were made to produce the Mk VIIM as were also given to the newly launched XK140, while the visual changes were small.

With the exception that the rear bumpers were now to be wrapped further around the flanks of the bodyshell, the only easy way to pick out the new Mk VIIM from a Mk VII was at the front. Here, the Lucas auxiliary lamps had been repositioned on the front apron instead of being flush mounted to the bodyshell. The shell itself was treated to a pair of chrome grilles which shielded the twin horns, while flashing indicators were fitted to the nose of the front wings, replacing the semaphores originally fitted to the B/C pillar between the door openings.

The output of the magnificent 3.4-litre twin-cam XK engine received its first official boost (tune-up kits had been available from the factory for some time, but not on a production-line basis), which was achieved by using higher-lift camshafts (which had ⅜in

(9mm) instead of 5⁄16in (8mm) peaks) and improved cylinder head porting. There was claimed to be no loss of low-speed flexibility.

According to Jaguar's official figures (which we have now learned to treat with caution!), here is a direct comparison:

Feature	Mk VII (gross)	Mk VIIM
Peak power	160bhp @ 5,200rpm	190bhp @ 5,500rpm
Peak torque	195lb/ft @ 2,500rpm	203lb/ft @ 3,000rpm

This equates to a 19 per cent increase in power output, but only a 4 per cent improvement in peak torque, which, in fact, made the latest XK engine more sporting and less overtly 'touring' than before. However, it was still so flexible and so much more efficient than almost every other production car engine, that its character change was freely accepted.

To match these changes, the internal gearbox ratios were modified – the new box, effectively, being a 'close ratio' unit – the same changes also being applied for the new XK140. At the same time, the front suspension was firmed up considerably by specifying larger diameter torsion bars. The wheel rate went up from 128lb/in to no less than 154lb/in, though even this could not be called 'stiff' by most standards.

Although the Mk VIIM still included some 'transatlantic' compromises which made British teeth grate a little – with automatic transmission there was the use of a bench

Jaguar introduced the Mk VIIM in 1954, a car which had very few style changes, but a significantly more powerful engine. At the front end the extra driving lamps were mounted on the apron instead of into the front panel itself, which left space for extra air intakes in the nose. The V-screen was retained.

front seat, along with an awful umbrella-handle handbrake control under the dashboard – it was still a very fast and attractive proposition. In fact, these snarls would have to remain theoretical at first, for automatic transmission was not available on domestic-market Mk VIIMs until the autumn of 1955, when it cost £181, a price hike of more than 10 per cent.

By this time, too, the much disliked British 'Restrictive Covenant' (which obliged new-car buyers to keep their cars for a minimum period before re-sale – latterly two years – as an enforced way to keep down the demand) had been abandoned, while deliveries to the British market had been allowed to build up. All this despite the fact that Jaguar production seemed to be

The contours of the Mk VII family style did not allow a very large boot, especially as the vertically mounted spare wheel took up a lot of space on the right side of the compartment.

stagnating, at about 10,000 cars a year of all types.

In the end this meant that the new Mk VIIM became much more familiar on British roads than the original Mk VII had been at first. Even so, Jaguar's own figures confirm that 7,930 Mk VIIs were originally sold in the UK, compared with 6,243 Mk VIIMs.

MK VIIM ON SALE

Although the magazines show that the Mk VIIM gave way to the Mk VIII in October 1956, many people forget that the Mk VIIM then stayed in production until the following summer, this being the first occasion that new and old types of this design were built side-by-side.

Once the Mk VIIM was officially released to the British market – the first batch were sent overseas – it rapidly took over from the Mk VII. Customers soon discovered that it was significantly faster than the original types, independent tests showing that the top speed had increased to about 105mph

Jaguar Mk VIIM (1954–7)

Numbers built
10,061

Engine
Type	Jaguar XK
Block material	Cast iron
Head material	Cast aluminium
Cylinders	6 in-line
Cooling	Water
Bore and stroke	83 x 106mm
Capacity	3,442cc
Main bearings	7
Valves	2 per cylinder, operated by twin ohc, and inverted bucket-type tappets
Compression ratio	8.0:1 (or optional 7.0:1 or 9.0:1)
Max. power	190bhp @ 5,500rpm (on 8.0:1 CR)
Max. torque	203lb/ft at 3,000rpm

Transmission
Clutch	Single dry plate; hydraulically operated

Internal gearbox ratios
Top	1.00
3rd	1.365
2nd	1.98
1st	3.37
Reverse	3.37
Final drive	4.27:1

Optional internal gear ratios
Top	1.00
3rd	1.21
2nd	1.75
1st	2.98
Reverse	2.98

Suspension and steering
Front	Independent, torsion bars, wishbones, anti-roll bar, telescopic dampers
Rear	Live (beam) axle, by half-elliptic leaf springs, telescopic dampers
Steering	Recirculating ball
Tyres	6.70–16in cross-ply
Wheels	Steel disc, bolt–on
Rim width	5.5in

Brakes
Type	Drum brakes at front and rear, hydraulically operated
Size	12in diameter drums

Dimensions
Track
Front	56.5 /1,435
Rear	58/1,473
Wheelbase	120/3,048
Overall length	196.5/4,991
Overall width	73.5/1,867
Overall height	62/1,575
Unladen weight	3,892lb/1,765kg

In the mid-1950s Jaguar's North American Corporation's New York showrooms attempted to recreate the British country house tradition. XK140 sports cars face the camera, and that is a Mk VIIM, complete with whitewall tyres, behind them.

(170km/h). For such a large car, too, it was still thought to be amazingly roadworthy, as North America's *Road & Track* confirmed: 'We will even say flatly that no American sedan car can keep up with the Mk VII over a crooked road'.

In addition, the Mk VII family continued to prove itself in motorsport, notably in saloon car racing and in the Monte Carlo rally. As described in Chapter 6, the rare appearances by the 'works' Jaguars always did marvellous things for the car's image. Even so, those seeking to identify trends should realize that Mk VIIM demand began to drop away almost as soon as the smaller 2.4-litre saloon model went on sale at the end of 1955. Quite simply, before then the Mk VII/Mk VIIM model had been the only Jaguar saloon car on the market, presumably one which was too large, ponderous and expensive for some.

Certainly Mk VIIM sales became harder to find during 1956 – especially as Britain's economic climate took a turn for the worse – and demand never really recovered to its early 1950s level.

MK VIII

The next update of a successful design came in the autumn of 1956, when the Mk VIIM was joined by a glitzier derivative, the Mk VIII; the two versions of the same car carried on in harness until the summer of 1957.

There was nothing revolutionary about the Mk VIII, for in most respects it was just the same as what had gone before. Compared with the Mk VIIM, it was made more powerful, better in several minor ways and given style changes to emphasize the message. It was almost as if the company had given the Mk VIIM a mid-life makeover.

So, after six years, Jaguar apparently still thought there was life in this Big Jaguar design. The recently knighted Sir William Lyons (this honour was confirmed in the New Year's Honours List of January 1956) might have liked to do more, but at this point in its history Jaguar was seriously overloaded with new products and projects.

The new monocoque 2.4 was about to be joined by the 3.4, the XK150 was about to replace the XK140 and a new E-Type race car was at the design stage. Already overwhelmed by this, Jaguar had recently withdrawn from motor racing, so there was no question of redesigning or replacing the Mk VII family at this moment in its history.

To turn the Mk VIIM into the Mk VIII, Jaguar gave the car a better and more powerful engine, changes were made to the transmission, improvements to the interior and, for the first and only time in the eleven-year history of this car, style changes to the exterior.

By adding a wide chrome decoration around the existing radiator grille, the front end of the car looked subtly different from before, in fact it some ways it looked rather like the Graber-styled Alvis saloons of the period. Duotone paintwork became standard, the two colours being separated along the flanks by chrome strips with a rather contrived line which followed the contours of the front wing/door bulges themselves. Finally, having originally chosen a shallow-angle V-screen for the Mk VII and Mk VIIMs, Jaguar finally fell into line with the rest of the industry by adopting a full-width, one-piece windscreen, though tiny changes to the sheet metalwork were never made to suit.

The major mechanical change was to the noble 3.4-litre XK engine, which was given a re-worked cylinder head, and a twin-pipe exhaust system. The head, later to become known as the B-Type, combined the enlarged inlet and exhaust valves of the C-Type race car with slightly smaller diameter inlet ports.

In the introduction of this engine there

While the Mk VIII and Mk IX saloons were in production, Jaguar also built the XK150 sports car. The disc brakes from this model, and some of the more powerful engine derivatives, were later standardized on the saloons too.

was a truly classic piece of Jaguar double-speak as far as power output was concerned; we now know that Jaguar never quoted anything remotely close to accurate figures for their power units at this time – but neither did their principal competitors in the United States, the American manufacturers! At first no power or torque improvements were claimed for the B-Type headed 3.4-litre, but once the new car was tested it was clear that a lot more power was being produced. Not daunted, Jaguar merely revised their quoted

peak outputs during 1957 – from 190bhp and 203lb/ft to 210bhp and 216lb/ft – and nothing further was said!

There was also an important improvement to the Borg Warner automatic transmission's installation, something which was developed by Jaguar and kept strictly to itself. This was the ability for the driver to hold the transmission in 'Intermediate' when he needed it most. Normally, on most automatic transmission cars, say, when they approached a corner in the intermediate

In the 1990s, I suppose, we would expect lights, indicators and air intakes all to be grouped together, but in the 1950s the Mk VIII was considered to be a particularly neat body style.

The Mk VIII looked nearly identical to earlier Mk VIIs and Mk VIIMs, except for the duotoning and cutaway wheel spats.

Compared with the Mk VIIM, the Mk VIII of 1956 had a one-piece screen, cutaway rear wheel spats, and a duotone colour scheme. In addition there was a bolder front radiator grille style than before.

range and the driver lifted his foot from the throttle, the transmission would automatically change up, which was potentially an unbalancing manoeuvre. Now for the Mk VIII, there was an extra flip switch provided on the facia panel, which the driver could operate if he wanted to hold that ratio.

That switch, known as 'intermediate hold', which was also an intermediate selector if required, would persist on this and other Jaguars for some years, though I am not sure that many drivers ever found time to operate it, especially on Mk VIIIs where the steering was so low-geared that their hands would usually be busy elsewhere!

Quite a lot of work had gone into upgrading the interior, notably at the rear where the back rests had been re-shaped to provide individually shaped squabs and there was a central, fold-down, arm rest. Fold-down polished wood picnic tables were also built in to the back of the front seats, something not previously available on Mk VIIMs.

Unhappily, if automatic transmission was specified, an unsupportive bench front seat came with it: those ordering manual (or manual plus overdrive) Mk VIIIs also got the pleasure of separate, though large, front seats instead.

Although the Mk VIII was more fully equipped than the Mk VIIM and therefore about 130lb heavier, it was even faster than before (which thoroughly discredited the

The Mk VIII's front end featured the same lamp/air intake positions as the Mk VIIM, but this time there was also a more prominent and more highly chromed radiator grille.

Jaguar Mk VIII (1956–9)

Numbers built
6,212

Layout
Box–section chassis frame with separate steel bodyshell. Five-seater, front engine/rear drive, sold as four-door saloon

Engine

Type	Jaguar XK
Block material	Cast iron
Head material	Cast aluminium
Cylinders	6 in–line
Cooling	Water
Bore and stroke	83 x 106mm
Capacity	3,442cc
Main bearings	7
Valves	2 per cylinder, operated by twin ohc, and inverted bucket-type tappets
Compression ratio	8.0:1 (or optional 7.0:1)
Carburettors	2 SU 1.75in
Max. power	210bhp @ 5,500rpm
Max. torque	216lb/ft @ 3,000rpm

Transmission
Four-speed manual gearbox, with synchromesh on top, third and second gears

Clutch	Single dry plate; hydraulically operated

Internal gearbox ratios

Top	1.00
3rd	1.365
2nd	1.98
1st	3.37
Reverse	3.37
Final drive	4.27:1

Overdrive (Laycock) was optional, on top gear only, when the final drive ratio became 4.55:1. Internal transmission ratio was:

Top (O/D)	0.778

Automatic transmission (Borg Warner) was optional. Internal gearbox ratios were:

Direct	1.00
Intermediate	1.44
Low	2.31
Reverse	2.0

| Maximum torque multiplication | 2.15 |
| Final drive ratio | 4.27:1 |

Suspension and steering

Front	Independent, torsion bars, wishbones, anti-roll bar, telescopic dampers
Rear	Live (beam) axle, by half-elliptic leaf springs, telescopic dampers
Steering	Recirculating ball
Tyres	6.70–16in cross-ply
Wheels	Steel disc, bolt-on
Rim width	5.5in

Brakes

| Type | Drum brakes at front and rear, hydraulically operated |
| Size | 12in diameter drums |

Dimensions

Track	
Front	56.5/1,435
Rear	58/1,473
Wheelbase	120/3,048
Overall length	196.5/4,991
Overall width	73.5/1,867
Overall weight	62/1,575
Unladen weight	4,032lb/1,829kg

idea that the B-Type cylinder head did not release more power than its predecessor!) and at this stage there were few cars to be seen on the roads that were more impressive than a Mk VIII in a hurry.

Very few big Jaguars appear to have been chauffeur-driven at this juncture, which is probably just as well, for rear-seat passengers would surely have been flung around by the way that many drivers seemed to drive these vast but surprisingly capable saloons.

These were the cars which lorded it over almost everything else on the first new-generation roads which started to be built in the UK at this time – or, for that matter, in Europe and the USA. Where conditions allowed it, 80mph (125km/h) or even 90mph (145km/h) was a relaxed cruising gait, for the top speed was around 107–109mph (172–175km/h).

This sort of performance was a great tribute to the fabulous XK engine, for with the automatic transmission most of these cars seemed to have, at 90mph (145km/h) the long-stroke design was turning over at 4,650rpm, something which would have been unheard of only ten years earlier.

In view of the Mk VIII's very large frontal area and an aerodynamic shape which, on reflection, has a barn-door-like appearance, the fact that something like 18mpg (16l/100km) could regularly be achieved was something of a miracle. Perhaps this explains why *The Autocar* felt able to describe the Mk VIII as: 'outstanding by any standards' and why a total of 6,212 cars – sometimes at a rate of around 100 cars a week – were built in less than three years.

Very few important technical improvements were made in that time, the most

Two aspects of access to the engine bay of a late 1950s Mk VIII, emphasizing not only the high, fixed sides, but also the width of the cavern. The XK engine was large, but very neatly detailed, there being a good deal of space at the exhaust side of the assembly.

This 1957 Mk VIII has separate front seats with fore-and-aft adjustment. Now compare it with ...

significant being the fitment of Burman power-assisted steering as an option, to a few left-hand-drive machines from April 1958. By that time, however, the Mk VIII was on the point of being rendered obsolete by yet another improvement on the same separate-chassis theme.

MK IX

As is made clear in Chapter 8, the Mk IX label should really have been applied to a new-style 'Big Jaguar' at the end of the 1950s, not to the last of the Mk VII family. William Lyons had started project work on a new 'Zenith' project in 1957/8, when it was always known, internally, as 'the new Mk IX', but there were so many delays in bringing that car to the market that the life of the Mk VIII had to be prolonged for a time. 'Zenith' eventually became Mk X and an interim Mk

... the bench seat and different fold-down table / storage arrangements of the ex-Queen Mother Mk VIIM / Mk IX model preserved in the Jaguar collection.

The notable Mk VIIM/Mk IX which was used by Her Majesty the Queen Mother for so many years, was always chauffeur-driven, featured automatic transmission and had a bench front seat usually set well forward to allow Her Majesty the maximum possible leg-room in the rear. When bench seats were fitted, the - umbrella-handle handbrake was always retained on these cars.

IX was hurried into the showrooms to hold the line.

The development period preceding the launch of the Mk IX, the last of the separate-chassis Big Jaguars, was quite astonishingly short. Certainly there was no thought of putting such a car on sale in the spring of 1958 when I first started to work in the Jaguar drawing offices, but it wasn't long before a quick programme went ahead and

the new car was introduced in October of the same year.

Even so, there was no master plan at first, which explains remarks overheard in the design offices such as: 'Oh yes, we're disc braking the Mk VIII for the Motor Show' and 'We'll probably try the 3.8-litre engine in the Mk VIII before we put it into the new Mk IIs'.

Certainly the pace of this makeover explains why there were absolutely no style changes – except, in fact, for the adoption of a 'Mk IX' badge on the tail. There simply wasn't time to tackle anything more. It also made it possible for Jaguar to continue the Mk VIII alongside the Mk IX for more than a year – Jaguar's planners could cope with the chassis differences, while Pressed Steel continued to supply identical bodyshells. The piercings for the 'Mk IX' badge were made at Browns Lane.

From memory, I believe this badge had to be sourced from Wilmot Breeden in Birmingham (a company from which Jaguar bought much of its brightwork) and that Lyons had to engage in some very special pleading to make sure the moulds could be tooled up, and supplies guaranteed, for Mk IX assembly to begin in October 1958!

The simplest way to describe a launch-specification Mk IX is as a Mk VIII with an enlarged engine, four-wheel disc brakes and power-assisted steering as standard equipment. In all other respects the bulk, the style, the weight and the character were unchanged from those of the Mk VIII.

THE FIRST ENLARGED XK ENGINES

Looking back, it seems to have taken a long time for Jaguar to enlarge the six-cylinder XK engine. North American rivals such as Cadillac, Lincoln and Chrysler seemed to be able to alter engine sizes more or less at will,

The Mk IX, launched in 1958, was the last of that particular line, looking virtually the same as the previous Mk VIII, though there was a discreet 'Mk IX' badge on the boot lid panel. Hidden behind those wheels, too, there were four-wheel disc brakes – the first time such brakes had been fitted as standard to 'Big Jaguars'.

but not Jaguar. For the first few years, at least, Bill Heynes's team concentrated on tuning up the legendary unit, rather than trying to make it larger.

In fact it was not at all easy to make the engine significantly larger, as Jaguar had discovered even before it was introduced. When Harry Weslake recommended a proto-type size increase – from 3.2-litres – he was told that there was not enough water between the barrels for that, for the cylinder bores were too close together. The capacity increase was achieved by increasing the stroke, something of which he (Weslake) did not approve.

In the end it was the relentless development of racing sports cars which made a larger engine inevitable. After only two

By the late 1950s Jaguar rev-counters had reverted to a conventional clockwise movement of their needles. The automatic transmission change quadrant was always positioned behind the steering wheel on these models.

years it was clear that the sleek and lovely D-Type would soon be overwhelmed by larger and larger-engined Ferraris and Maseratis. Over in the United States in 1956, Alfred Momo (a company which prepared racing cars for Briggs Cunningham), enlarged two 'works'-loaned units by boring out the cylinder blocks by 0.170in (4.3mm). This conversion was believed to be such a success that an engine was returned to the UK for testing, was found to be reliable, and similar engines were subsequently adopted for use in some 1957 racing D-Types.

Once a 3.8-litre-equipped car had domi-

nated at Le Mans in that year, winning the marque's fifth 24 Hour Race in seven years, production-standard units were speedily developed, featuring press-fit dry liners for the first time in this engine. A simple bore increase of 4mm was chosen, the cylinder block castings were lightly modified and the well-known capacity of 3,781cc was the result. Ever afterwards it became known as the '3.8'-litre unit, that size being cast into the walls of the cylinder block.

By 1958 Jaguar had decided to use this enlarged engine in a variety of cars – Mk 2 saloon, E-Type sports car and Mk X among them – but it made its world-wide debut in the Mk IX in October 1958. Nominally this had 220bhp and a peak torque of 240lb/ft, which compared with 210bhp and 216lb/ft for the last of the 3.4-litre engines fitted to the Mk VIII. Nowadays, of course, we know that these were 'gross' figures and that the flywheel outputs were considerably less than that. Even so, on the basis of these figures there was a very worthwhile torque increase of 11 per cent, almost exactly in line with the capacity increase itself.

Compared with the original 3.4-litre engine, other consequential changes were few, though lead-bronze crankshaft bearings were specified and there was a new type of cold-start ('automatic choke') device in the SU carburettor installation. As ever, there was to be a choice of transmissions: manual transmission, by way of the ageing Moss-type four-speed gearbox, a manual plus over-drive option, or the use of Borg Warner Type DG three-speed automatic transmission.

Except in detail, the new disc brake installation was like that of the latest XK150 sports cars, which was reasonable as that car still shared the same front suspension and rear axle designs as the big saloons. As a graduate engineer, in the chassis drawing office, I recall helping to draw up the assembly scheme for the Mk IX system, using an XK150 drawing as a crib sheet!

The third major innovation was the fitment of Burman power-assisted steering as standard, the same installation as offered on a few export-market Mk VIIIs earlier in 1958. By modern standards this system was no great shakes, as it lacked the precision of a rack-and-pinion layout, but at least it allowed the steering ratio to be changed (there were three and a half turns from lock-to-lock) and its operation was almost finger light.

Jaguar Mk IX (1958–61)

Numbers built
10,009

Layout
Box-section chassis frame with separate steel bodyshell. Five-seater, front engine/rear drive, sold as four-door saloon

Engine

Type	Jaguar XK
Block material	Cast iron
Head material	Cast aluminium
Cylinders	6 in-line
Cooling	Water
Bore and stroke	87 x 106mm
Capacity	3,781cc
Main bearings	7
Valves	2 per cylinder, operated by twin overhead camshafts, and inverted bucket-type tappets
Compression ratio	8.0:1 (or optional 7.0:1)
Carburettors	2 SU 1.75in
Max. power	220bhp @ 5,500rpm
Max. torque	240lb/ft @ 3,000rpm

Transmission
Four-speed manual gearbox, with synchromesh on top, third and second gears.

Clutch   Single dry plate; hydraulically operated

Internal gearbox ratios
Top   1.00
3rd   1.365
2nd   1.98
1st   3.37
Reverse   3.37
Final drive   4.27:1

Overdrive (Laycock) was optional, on top gear only, when the final drive ratio became 4.55:1. Internal transmission ratio was:

Top (O/D)   0.778

Automatic transmission (Borg Warner) was optional. Internal gearbox ratios were:

Direct   1.00
Intermediate   1.44
Low   2.31
Reverse   2.0
Maximum torque
   multiplication   2.15
Final drive ratio   4.27:1

Suspension and steering
Front   Independent, torsion bars, wishbones, anti-roll bar, telescopic dampers
Rear   Live (beam) axle, by half-elliptic leaf springs, telescopic dampers
Steering   Recirculating ball, power-assisted
Tyres   6.70–16in cross-ply
Wheels   Steel disc, bolt-on
Rim width 5.5in

Brakes
Type   Disc brakes at front and rear, with vacuum servo assistance
Size   12.125in diameter front, 12in diameter rear

Dimensions (in/mm)
Track
   Front   56.5/1,435
   Rear   58/1,473
Wheelbase   120/3,048
Overall length   196.5/4,991
Overall width   73.5/1,867
Overall height   62/1,575
Unladen weight   3,980lb/1,807kg

But with no visual changes, few revisions to the interior (except for a more powerful heating system) and the same large, stately, sometimes daunting character, what was the public to make of the Mk IX? Jaguar, in fact, had taken a big gamble by keeping the Mk VIII in production, then applying a significant price increase for the Mk IX. At Motor Show time in October 1958, this is how the prices compared:

Mk VIII (manual transmission), £1,830;
Mk VIII (automatic transmission), £1,998;
Mk IX (manual transmission), £1,995;
Mk IX (automatic transmission), £2,163.

This meant that, model for model, 3.8-litres plus disc brakes plus power-assisted steering cost £165, or an extra 9 per cent. In fact the automatic transmission Mk IX was the first ever Jaguar to be priced at more than £2,000, and one or two gloom-mongers thought this could have been a problem to the Coventry concern. In fact it was a gamble which worked. In the end the Mk IX was built from October 1958 to September 1961, during which time 10,009 examples were produced, of which 5,362 were sold in the UK. That equates to about 300 cars built every month, not a figure likely to cause much excitement to companies like Ford and General Motors,

When Jaguar adopted Borg Warner automatic transmission as optional equipment, it also developed the then-unique 'intermediate hold' feature, which was controlled by this switch, positioned on the facia panel close to the driver's hands.

but one quite high enough to make Jaguar's British rivals very jealous indeed.

In fact it was the combination of the old Mk IX and the new compact Mk2 Jaguars which finally killed off one of Jaguar's last potential rivals – Armstrong-Siddeley – for the Sapphire, a straight competitor to the Mk VII/VIII/IX family, simply could not match the Jaguars for value.

From my privileged position inside Jaguar at the time, I spent many an hour in the Mk IX. Even though I was young, arrogant and totally smitten by the idea of the forthcoming E-Type sports car, I still enjoyed driving any Mk IX, which was very quick, quiet and still surprisingly manoeuvrable.

I didn't enjoy the automatic transmission versions (most cars destined for the USA were so equipped) as much as the manual plus overdrive types, but that was mainly because of the wide and very slippery front bench seats which were standard on those cars. Nor did I like the steering, if only because it didn't seem to be very precise and was lacking in feel. A look at the complex linkage will help to show why this was so. Indeed, with the cross-ply tyres of the day, there was sometimes an eerie feeling that (as a Coventry-based Godiva Car Club member once used to describe it):

There's some elastic somewhere in there. The big round wheel in the cockpit isn't really connected to the big round wheels on the ground at the front!

That was an exaggeration, but there was no doubt that the Mk IX driver had to work away quite hard on undulating or uneven road surfaces if he was going to keep the car in a totally straight line.

The brakes, though, were a complete revelation. As a co-driver I had just got used to the stopping power of rally cars like the TR3A, but to experience the same thing on a big and heavy saloon car was quite miracu-

lous. In normal conditions it seemed that I could hit the pedal hard, again and again, without any sign of the stopping power disappearing. The handbrake, though, was different. Whichever Dunlop engineer thought that the (separate) cheap and cheerful mechanical linkage would work consistently was suffering from gross over-optimism.

As ever, British motoring magazines were kind to the latest Jaguar, though careful reading confirmed what most early customers were already finding and when I saw them I was relieved to see that my own impressions were also backed.

By almost any contemporary standard, of course, this was still a remarkably fast car. How many other 4,000lb (1800kg) cars of this period could reach around 115mph (177km/h), still perform with honour on race tracks if asked, yet carry five or even six people in great comfort – all at a selling price of little more than £2,000? In Britain not one of Rover, Humber, Armstrong-Siddeley, or even the last of the six-cylinder Rolls-Royce Silver Clouds could beat the Big Jaguar in traffic light Grands Prix. In Continental Europe, too, there was only one serious contender – Mercedes-Benz – and their fuel-injected 3-litre saloons were not yet ready for sale.

This meant was that very few saloon cars (except other Jaguars, notably the 3.4 and 3.8 Mk IIs) could keep up with hard-driven Mk VIIIs and Mk IXs, so unless owners were worried about heavy fuel consumption, they could reign supreme.

Fuel consumption was poor for the Mk IXs; even with manual transmission and overdrive, they could rarely beat 14–15mpg (19.9–20.2l/100km). *Autocar's* 1958 automatic-transmission test car achieved 14.4mpg (19.6l/100km), which was predictable enough, but the same test reported that at a constant speed of 80mph (130km/h) the result was 15.2mpg (18.6l/100km), while at a steady 100mph (160km/h) it was an awful 11.5mpg (24.6l/100km).

Although the same test noted that the Mk IX 'when roused, can accelerate like a sports car' and that 'the joy of disc brakes lies in their ability to continue receiving hard punishment with scarcely appreciable fade', it was clear that its time was nearly up. On the one hand, '... the Jaguar Mk IX surely provides more of the requirements for rapid and effortless travel than any of its commercial competitors', but there was also the reminder that 'although this largest Jaguar is based on a design introduced back in 1950, progressive development has kept it abreast of the times'.

By this time, in fact, the basic design (which dated from 1947/8) was already a decade old, and in some ways this particular Jaguar was already well out of date. Although it still looked graceful, fashion conscious clientele (especially in the USA) who might have been in line for a new car were beginning to desert a breed of which they might have owned three or even four already.

Jaguar, of course, was already wise to this problem, and a totally new structure, to become the Mk X model, was already on the way. Assembly of Mk IXs tailed off in the summer of 1961 and ended immediately before the Mk X was launched. In eleven years, a total of 47,190 of this family were produced.

6 Racing and Rallying

Today's enthusiasts may well look at these Jaguars – large, heavy and not easy to drive flat out – and wonder how they could possibly have been race or rally winners in the 1950s.

It is fact, however, that not only were Mk VIIs and Mk VIIMs the pace setters in Touring Car racing at the time, but they also won the Monte Carlo rally, and so nearly won this famous event twice. The grace and the space had nothing to do with this record, but the pace most certainly did. At a time when there was no such thing as a specially designed 'homologation special', the Jaguars' main advantage was always their powerful and torquey engines.

RALLYING WITH THE 3½-LITRE

When the 3½-litre saloon was launched in 1937, rallies could be won by accurate time-keeping and by a car's performance on the manoeuvring tests. Smaller cars – particularly smaller sports cars – usually took most of the awards, which explains why the SS100 was a favourite machine.

Northerner Jack Harrop won the RAC rally in 1937 in an SS100, and soon after 3½-litre saloon deliveries began, Jaguar lent him a factory car (DHP 736) for the 1938 event. Many of the RAC rallies of the 1930s were long drawn-out and tedious events, only enlivened by the driving test at the end, but this was not the case in April/May 1938.

Two hundred and thirty-seven cars started from five points – Glasgow, Harrogate,

Leamington Spa, London and Torquay – then completed more than 1,000 miles, which for all included climbing the Bwlch-y-Groes and Honister passes. All this, at an average running speed of 26mph, without rest halts, in cars without heaters or reclining seats, meant there was no time to catch up on any sleep. The cavalcade of exhausted drivers eventually reached Blackpool, and the finish, where there were three high-speed manoeuvring tests on the promenade.

On one of these complicated tests, incidentally, the clock started running with the driver outside the car, with the engine switched off. *The Autocar* noted just how far SS's preparation had clearly gone because: 'Harrop, whose SS had a queer device which started the engine when the driver opened the door, was absolutely terrific, in spite of a bad skid when reversing ...'.

Harrop, flinging the 125bhp saloon around as if it was a sports car (no power steering, no disc brakes, remember), was within fractions of setting fastest times on all three tests. When the results were calculated, the 3½-litre not only won its class (incidentally, beating Leslie Johnson and Hugh Hunter's Frazer-Nash-BMWs in the process!), but won Britain's prestigious event outright.

Harrop, who also set a sturdy performance in the Monte Carlo rally of 1939 in another Coventry-registered car (DKV 101), when he finished tenth-equal overall and attained 'Best British Car' performance, was clearly at his peak in the 1930s, as was the 3½-litre, for by the time rallying got back into its swing after the Second World War this model was obsolete.

There was, however, just one intriguing postscript. In 1947, frustrated by the time it took for peace-time Europe to get back to normal, *The Motor*'s sports editor, Rodney Walkerley, mounted his own private Monte Carlo rally. 'The idea came quite suddenly when we were bemoaning the absence of the Monte Carlo rally from the 1947 fixture list.' Inviting fellow Monte enthusiast Mike Couper to accompany him, and having borrowed a brand-new Jaguar 3½-litre from the factory, he set out to recreate the winter classic – all on his own.

FVC 879 set out from austerity-riddled London on 27 January, crossed the stormy English Channel via ferry to Calais, then tackled a self-imposed pre-war type of Monte schedule through Le Mans to Bordeaux, then Le Puy, Lyons and Grenoble, before fighting its way through the mountains to Nice and Monte Carlo itself.

There were no prizes, of course – and no witnesses – but the result was a fascinating written feature noting the awful conditions, the temporary bridges (by-passing war damage) which had to be crossed, the constant search for petrol, food and permits. Just a jolly? Maybe, but if this was a winter holiday, it was certainly different and at least: 'Owing to the standardization of an interior heater, our personal comfort was assured …'.

With only one minor 'cheat' – a stop for six hours' rest in a Lyons hotel – the intrepid crew arrived outside the Hotel Metropole in Monte Carlo, 1,310 miles from where they had started, after 52hr 15min; 2hr 15min late on their original imposed schedule. As Walker later wrote in *The Motor*:

> The Jaguar, of course, aroused immense interest and wherever we parked (it having been beautifully washed and polished) small groups assembled and gave vent to expressions of approval. Its splendid lines and impressive appearance were not lost upon an audience which knows a fine car when it sees one …
>
> Only a very good car could possibly have got through under the really bad conditions we encountered, and the great power of the Jaguar was at a premium in forcing its way at low rpm in second and third gear over the snowbound passes without impossible wheelspin.
>
> Of course, we were never able to use anything like maximum speed, although, on the run home, we speedometered an easy 95mph with revs in hand … The Jaguar returned to this country after a drive back over snow and ice the whole way, smooth, silent and 'without a hair out of place'....

RALLYING IN THE 1950s

By comparison with what was to come, the 3½-litre cars' exploits, of course, were mere sideshows. Since the first post-war RAC rally was not held until 1951 and since the Monte was only revived in 1949, the new Mk V had little chance to make its sporting reputation. Of 282 starters, only two new privately entered 3½-litre Mk Vs tackled the 1950 Monte (Messrs Rockman and Warwick both started from Glasgow).

A year later the Mk V, already made obsolete by the launch of the Mk VII, nearly made history, for Cecil Vard of Northern Ireland took his own car (ZE 7445) into a fine third place overall, beaten only by Trevoux's Delahaye sports saloon and Comte de Monte Real's 3.9-litre Ford V8.

Another Mk V, driven by Wally Waring and Jaguar dealer Wilf Wadham, finished ninth. Both on the Monaco GP circuit test, where the big saloon rolled considerably on corners, but did not let go, and in the driving test, Vard's Mk V was outstanding. Remember that this was a big and heavy car, on cross-ply tyres, with low-geared steering and that Vard was paying his own bills!

117

That, incidentally, was not quite the end of a competition career for the Mk V, for in 1953 Cecil Vard entered the same Irish 1950-registered car again, when it finished in a magnificent fifth place.

In the meantime, the XK-engined Mk VII had arrived, and before long it had started to appear in rallies where performance, rather than nippiness around pylons in driving tests, was an advantage. Most Jaguar enthusiasts, in any case, chose to run XK120s, which were a lot lighter and faster, but for certain events the Mk VII was very suitable.

In the 1952 Monte Carlo rally Jaguar dealer Ian Appleyard was not able to use his famous XK120 (the regulations required four-seater saloons to be employed) so instead he took a newly prepared Mk VII (PNW 7). Jaguar lent a 'works' car (LWK 343 – which would also be a 'works' race car in Silverstone events!) to Raymond Baxter, who was reporting on the event for the BBC, while OKV 76 was driven by Bob Berry and Alan Currie as a support car.

Although privately entered Mk VIIs finished fourth and sixth in this Monte, the 'works' aided efforts came to nothing, and LWK 343 did not figure in the results of the RAC rally, where it had been loaned to journalist Tommy Wisdom. Ian and Mrs Pat Appleyard, once again driving PNW 7, finished an absolutely storming second overall in the Dutch Tulip rally, close behind Ken Wharton's 'works' Ford Consul which beat the Jaguar on a manoeuvring test, though Appleyard was easily faster on the Zandvoort racing circuit speed trial.

A year later Ian Appleyard came within one second of winning the Monte Carlo rally in PNW 7, for this was the event settled by a competitor's 'regularity' on the 46-mile loop in the mountains behind the Principality, which included a climb and descent of the narrow, hairpin-riddled and icy Col de Braus. No fewer than 404 cars started this event, of which 253 finished unpenalized on the 2,000-mile road section, and eight Jaguars qualified to tackle the last test.

Stirling Moss enjoyed racing the 'works' Mk VIIs, even though their suspension was very soft. LKW 343 carried racing number 30 at Silverstone in May 1952, when it lapped in 2 min 18 sec.

Having practised the mountain circuit, the 'works' backed crews were all nearly perfect on the icy regularity sections. In the end, that wily old campaigner Maurice Gatsonides lost a mere two seconds in his Ford Zephyr, to win the event, while the Appleyards lost three seconds. By one second, the mere blink of an eye, the Mk VII was 'robbed' of a great victory.

Jaguar (Appleyard, Vard and Bennett) won the team prize. Incidentally there were four Jaguars in the top fifteen places, including Air-Vice-Marshal Don Bennett eighth, with a still relatively unknown driver called Ronnie Adams of Northern Ireland in fifteenth place. Jaguar fans would come to know more about him in years to come.

With the exception of Appleyard's hardworking Mk VII winning its class in the Tulip rally, and taking fifth overall, the rest of the rallying year was quiet for the Mk VII and by 1954 – when new sports cars like the TR2 made many headlines – the Big Jaguars were already beginning to look rather old-fashioned, even cumbersome. Even so, Ronnie Adams finished sixth on the Monte in his own Mk VII, while Cecil Vard took eighth in a loaned 'works' car (LWK 343

– which was already a successful *Daily Express* racing saloon!).

For 1955 there was a strong line-up of Mk VIIs in the Monte, for Jaguar loaned PWK 700 to Ronnie Adams, Cecil Vard had PWK 701, while Ian and Pat Appleyard entered a new Leeds-registered car of their own, SUM 7. With Adams eighth and with these three cars winning the highly prized Charles Faroux Trophy (the team prize), all the effort was worthwhile, even though the Appleyard car blew an engine core plug on the mountain circuit close to the finish.

Then came 1956, a year in which the Adams–Mark VIIM combination excelled itself by winning the Monte Carlo outright, against all the odds! Three cars – all seasoned 'works'; race or rally cars – were prepared at Browns Lane:

PWK 700	Ronnie Adams/Frank Biggar/Derek Johnston
LWK 343	Cecil Vard/Arthur Jolley/ Jimmy Millard
OVC 69	Reg Mansbridge/Joan Mansbridge/P. Strawson

Ronnie Adams on his way to winning the Monte Carlo Rally of 1956 in PWK 700, which also found time to be a 'works' race car at Silverstone.

LWK 343 was a Jaguar development car which was occasionally allowed out to win the Daily Express *Production Touring Car Race. Fitted with as many modifications as the regulations would allow (and a few more that Team Manager 'Lofty' England added anyway!) and with rear wheel spats removed, it was considerably faster than a standard car. Even so, it had to make do with drum brakes and rather soft suspension.*

As it turned out, this was a Monte with surprisingly mild weather, so all three 'Classification Tests' – which included a downhill speed and braking test on the Mont des Mules, and a difficult Mountain Circuit run in the Alpes Maritimes and taking in the Col du Turini (which is still a famous Monte special stage) – had a great bearing on the final positions.

Remarkably, Ronnie Adams's Mk VIIM was second fastest overall on the speed and braking test, then on the Mountain Circuit he put up a staggeringly competent show to win from Walter Schock's 'works' Mercedes-Benz 220. This is easy enough to write, but it underestimates the effort Adams must have put in to keep the big 4,000lb Jaguar between the snow banks and for Messrs Biggar and Johnston to keep up with the navigation and time keeping. (There were no studded tyres in those days.)

That was as good a way as any for the Mk VIIM to reach the zenith of its rallying career. Shortly it would be out-gunned by the smaller 3.4-litre saloon, but in any case rallying changed so much in the next few years that one needed either a sports car or an 'homologation special' saloon to be victorious.

RACING THE MK VIIS

It is difficult for today's racing enthusiasts to visualize a motor racing scene without saloon cars. Nowadays, ten or more manufacturers enter heavily sponsored teams of cars in the British Touring Car Championship, the drivers command very high fees to race them and millions of people watch their efforts on TV spectaculars, yet in the 1950s it was all very different.

Before 1952, in fact, Britain simply never saw any prestigious saloon car racing at all and even events for production sports cars were few and far between. By that time, however, the *Daily Express* had come to sponsor one of the country's most important racing weekends, the International Trophy

At Silverstone in May 1955, Jimmy Stewart (Jackie's elder brother) drove this 'works' Mark VIIM into second place at the Silverstone Touring Car race...

...but surely he was lapping the Ford Anglia for the first, or maybe second time at this point? PWK 700 was versatile, for eight months later it won the Monte Carlo rally in Ronnie Adams's hands.

race at Silverstone. The main event, naturally, was always for Grand Prix racing cars, but in 1952, for the first time, it was supported by a seventeen-lap (50 mile) saloon car race, which brought the crowd to its feet. This immediately became the highlight of the saloon racing year, for there would be no British Saloon Car Championship in Britain until 1958.

Since the technology of racing saloons had not even been considered, let alone devel-

oped, Jaguar, never slow to see the chance of a publicity coup if it was offered, prepared an ex-Monte/ex-RAC rally Mk VII (LWK 343) for Stirling Moss to drive. With the exceptions that it had a close-ratio XK120-type gearbox, a 4.27:1 axle ratio and stiffened up suspension, it was virtually standard. It now seems remarkable that there were no radial ply tyres, no power steering and the drum brakes were always likely to fade away. It was certainly an heroic effort.

Jaguar Mk VIIs, not only driven by Moss, but by Leslie Johnson and Bertie Bradnack, started as clear favourites, for the only other 3-litre-plus car was an Allard driven by Sydney Allard himself. Surprisingly, although Moss practised in 2 minutes 19 seconds, his Mk VII time was beaten by Ken Wharton's Healey Elliott, which was two seconds quicker than that.

Nineteen cars started (though Leslie Johnson's Mk VII did not). After tractor tycoon Harry Ferguson dropped the flag there was a Le Mans-style start in which the drivers ran across the road to their cars, which were parked against the pit walls, fired them up, then snaked away. Moss, practised, keen and expert at this type of start, was fast away and after one lap was being closely followed by Wharton's Healey, Allard's Allard and Grace's Riley 2½-litre saloon.

The Mk VII eventually lapped in 2min 18sec (76.36mph (123km/h)), and gradually pulled away from the Healey to win by 13.8 seconds. Bertie Bradnack's Mk VII (his own business car) finished fourth – a long way back, after a slow start, which was not helped by the fact that Bertie was a large man who did not excel at driver sprints and Le Mans starts!

Right from the start this was obviously a crowd-pleasing business, as *The Autocar*'s report made clear:

> In a very short time the crowd at the start let out an appreciative roar as Moss came round Woodcote in the lead – but the roar was for the way it was done: Moss used every inch of the road and some of the grass, too, putting the massive Mk VII into a terrific four-wheel drift, thereafter tearing past the pits in a cloud of dust ....

This race set a pattern which Jaguar was delighted to endorse, for every May for the next ten years a Jaguar of one type or another would start favourite, win, look spectacular in the process, and give the crowds plenty to talk about on the way home. In some ways it must have been wonderful for Jaguar's image, even though there were still some killjoys who thought it was a tad undignified for cars like the Mk VIIs to be thrown about in such an extrovert manner. Whatever, the Mk VIIs and Mk VIIMs won every *Daily Express* Saloon Car race from 1952 to 1956, before handing over to the 3.4-litre (later 3.8-litre) compact monocoque saloons to go even faster than before.

Sir William, who was never known to throw away money that could be saved, clearly thought it was all worthwhile and for the 1953 *Daily Express* race he once again hired Stirling Moss to drive LWK 343, an all-purpose development/rally car which became a racing star just once a year. Since there was no Healey opposition, Moss had an easier time than in 1952, lapping at precisely the same speed (2 min 18 sec), but winning by nearly a whole minute (in seventeen laps!) from Grace's Riley 2½-litre.

Perhaps it was all beginning to look too easy, and so for the 1954 *Daily Express* race Jaguar entered two cars and encouraged rally driver Ian Appleyard to enter his own rally car (SUM 7) as competition, as did Ronnie Adams (OZ 9499). Once again Stirling Moss used LWK 343 (which surely had every right to have been retired by this time!), while Tony Rolt drove LHP 5, another old development/test car.

The regulations being so free and easy (they called for what the FIA described as 'Special Series Touring Cars'), engines close to C-Type specification were fitted, developing about 200bhp and the cars were expected to be faster than before.

Following the drivers' sprint across the road, in the Le Mans-style start, Stirling Moss found that his engine's starter motor had jammed, which meant that Ian Appleyard soon took over the lead, which he

LWK 343 at Silverstone on its way to winning one of the Daily Express *Production Car Races. On this occasion Stirling Moss was the driver and, amazingly enough, he was not carrying his habitual 'Lucky 7' competition number! Over the years, Mk VII lap speeds at Silverstone were reduced by 9 seconds.*

held to the finish. By rocking the heavy car to and fro, Moss freed the starter, fired up after a 20-second delay and got going, well in arrears, then moved swiftly up through the field.

After only five laps (by which time Sims's 2½-litre Riley and Tony Crook's Lancia had both spun off), the Mk VIIs were back in 1-2-3 formation – Appleyard, Tony Rolt, Moss – which they held to the end. Appleyard's seventeen-lap race time was 36 seconds faster than that of Moss in 1953. Moss had lapped at an impressive 2 min 13 sec in practice, but all three Mk VIIs circulated at 2 min 16 sec in the race itself, two seconds a lap faster than in 1952 and 1953.

Autosport's Gregor Grant thought this was great stuff for:

At the risk of shocking the Formula-fervid, one is tempted to suggest that the Production Touring Car Race was the best spectacle of the day. From the breathtaking start (reminiscent of Hyde Park Corner at 5.05pm) to the Jaguars' triumphant finish, it was packed with interest … someone was

always lapping someone else; tyres were squealed or wheels lifted high in the air – and the crowd loved it.

This, in fact, was one of the very first saloon car races I ever witnessed and I back everything which Gregor wrote. It wasn't just that the Mk VIIs won, but the way they won. To see not one, but three, of these very large saloons appear over the brow from Abbey Curve before they braked for Woodcote (still a sweeping curve in those days), then to see them heel over alarmingly, bellowing and squealing their Dunlop racing tyres was a sight to remember. That, and the smell of tortured rubber they left behind after they had swept off under the bridge on the start-finish line, towards Copse Corner.

But maybe it was too easy. On the evidence of that 1-2-3 success and the way that Stirling Moss had scorched up through the field to sit obediently behind the other two Mk VIIs, it certainly looked like it. For the 1955 *Daily Express* event, though, Jaguar entered no fewer than three cars: 'old faithful' LWK 343, plus two of the ex-Monte Carlo

PWK 701 was driven into third place at the Silverstone Touring Car Race in May 1955, piloted by Desmond Titterington. Michael Burn's DKW respectfully makes room for the Jaguar to lap it in the inside at Copse.

'works' rally Mk VIIMs, PWK 700 and PWK 701. These Mk VIIs were nothing if not versatile, and on this occasion they were driven by Mike Hawthorn, Jimmy Stewart and Desmond Titterington. Ian Appleyard, hoping to repeat his 1954 success, entered his own white rally car.

Continuing development (and very lax regulations) saw the 'works' engines boosted to no less than 219bhp, which was achieved with D-Type cylinder heads, 9.0:1 compression ratios and all related details, a competition clutch, a close-ratio gearbox, high geared steering and stiffened suspension, not forgetting Dunlop racing tyres.

In the race it was only ever a matter of which Jaguar beat all the others for outright victory. Once the race had started, according to *Autosport*: '... 28 drivers galloped across the road; there was the patter of tiny feet, the slamming of doors and the pit area became like a speeded-up film of Hyde Park Corner at rush hour'.

Hawthorn was already in the lead at the end of the first of twenty-five laps and was never headed. The only casualty among the Jaguars was Appleyard's machine, whose engine expired in a cloud of steam (thus repeating its failure on the Monte Carlo rally). The three 'works' cars merely pulled further and further away from the rest of the field.

Hawthorn won easily in the venerable LWK 343, which made up for his disappointment earlier in the day, when the top radiator water hose on his D-Type blew out. As expected the other Big Jaguars finished second and third, 2 and 16 seconds behind Hawthorn respectively. The pace had increased yet again, for Hawthorn's fastest lap was 2 min 10 sec (81.06mph (130.5km/h)) – which was a massive eight seconds faster than the same old car had achieved three years earlier.

The story was still not quite complete, for two Mk VIIMs were entered for the 1956

Daily Express race, to be driven by Ivor Bueb and Paul Frère. Bueb used OVC 69, an ex-Monte Carlo rally car, and both were modified just about as far (maybe even further, knowing the attention 'Lofty' England gave to these events!) as the letter of the regulations would allow.

For once the Mk VIIMs were almost overlooked in the run up to the race, for Jaguar had also prepared one of the new monocoque 2.4 saloons, this machine being allocated to Mike Hawthorn, while Jaguar dealers John Coombs and Duncan Hamilton also entered 2.4s. Due to its superior handling and manoeuvrability, Hawthorn's car was faster than the Mk VIIMs in practice – at 2 min 7 sec it took pole position – but its engine broke a valve spring after only two laps.

Thereafter Bueb's Mk VIIM took the lead but was always strongly challenged by Ken Wharton's 'works' Austin A90 Westminster (which was as near to being a four-door Austin-Healey 100-Six with Weber carburettors as made no difference!). Although the impressive and extrovert A90 briefly took the lead on several occasions, it was the Mk VIIM which won the race – by just one second. Hamilton's 2.4 finished third, with Frére's Mk VIIM behind him.

Both the Mk VIIM and the A90 lapped in 2 min 9 sec, which meant that, all in all, there had been a 9 second improvement in five years. Although some of this improvement was due to chassis changes, much of the credit must go to more powerful engines and increasingly non-standard specifications.

Although *Autosport*'s race report was adulatory ('A great deal of awe was inspired on this occasion by the battle for first place between Ivor Bueb in the works Mk VII Jaguar and Ken Wharton in the much modified Austin Westminster ...'), John Bolster, writing on other pages, was clearly disillusioned by the way development had progressed:

Since Jaguar had built up such a formidable sports car racing record in the early 1950s, it was simple enough to use C-type (shown here) and D-type engine and transmission technology in the Mk VIIs where the regulations allowed this.

I decline to comment on the so-called touring car race. When regulations permit bonnets full of Weber carburettors, racing cylinder heads, and so forth, the thing can only become a farce. Boy, bring me my fuel-injection, twin-cam, 'Popular'!

Little did Bolster know (and Jaguar certainly did not admit it) that even more extreme measures had been considered for the 1954 *Daily Express* race, when Jaguar built an aluminium-bodied Mk VII – not just one with a few aluminium panels, but with an all-aluminium shell!

This was apparently commissioned in the winter of 1953/4 because the 'Coventry grapevine' suggested that lightweight versions of the new Armstrong-Siddeley 3.4-litre Sapphire might be built to win such races. In

response, Jaguar obtained three complete sets of aluminium body panels from Pressed Steel, and one complete aluminium shell was produced in the experimental department; other panels were held in reserve.

As already reported, 1954 was the year in which 'ordinary' Mk VIIs were used and won the Touring Car Race. At that stage the aluminium shell was not fitted to a race car, probably because the regulations for the event did not allow it to be used. Instead the shell was fitted to KRW 621, which had originally been delivered to Sir William Lyons himself in 1951. From 1954 this car inherited the aluminium shell, was then used as a development car and was finally sold off to Jaguar's Bob Berry. After using it as a racing saloon, an occasional rally car, and as a tow car for his caravan, Berry eventually

Ivor Bueb's Mk VIIM (OVC 69) came very close to being beaten in the 1956 Silverstone Touring Car race, for Ken Wharton's highly modified Austin A90 Westminster led to on several occasions. In the end, Bueb had to lap in 2min 9sec, and beat the A90 by a mere one second: it was the last such vistory for Mk VII-based cars, as the smaller and faster Jaguars 3.4s took over in 1957.

sold it. Re-registered (as EXA 99) and restored, it still survives.

The regulations were eventually tightened up for 1957, but by that time the Mk VIIM had already reached the end of the road as a competition car. For 1957 the 2.4 was joined by the 3.4, which soon became a formidable racing saloon car, even with drum brakes. Even in its first year, Mike Hawthorn's car lapped in 2 min 5 sec. By this time, too, the career of the 'works' Jaguars was officially over, though the factory continued to advise, prepare and loan cars for favoured customers in the next few years. In October 1956 a carefully worded press release stated that:

Jaguar Cars Ltd, after very serious consideration, announce their withdrawal from the field of international racing and other competitive events, and state that no official entries or works teams will be entered for events on the 1957 calendar.

The information gained as a result of the highly successful racing programme which the Company has undertaken in the past five years has been of utmost value, and much of the knowledge derived from racing experience has been applied to the development of the Company's product.

This neatly drew a line under the motor sport career of the Big Jaguars, which had started out being dominant when the car's advanced specification was enough to ensure victory, but had struggled more and more over the years. Everyone agreed, though, that it was remarkable that such large, heavy and, frankly, not very nimble machines could win in rallies and on the track. The versatility of the 'works' Mk VIIs, of course, was never in doubt, for several machines had appeared at Silverstone and taken part in the Monte Carlo rally, with distinction in all cases. It was a remarkable, if short-lived, story.

7 Jaguar in the 1950s and 1960s

Looking back from the 1990s, it would be easy, maybe too easy, to criticize Jaguar for the way it allowed the 'Big Jaguar' line to develop. But to do so would be to make two very big mistakes – to assume that Sir William Lyons had nothing else to think about throughout all these years and to assume that he was blessed with second sight! Pundits and historians, of course, are blessed with hindsight, which makes criticism and second-guessing very easy.

If Lyons had only had to think about the Big Jaguar saloons, it would have been easy to raise several major queries about his strategy. Why did the Mk VII not arrive until five years after the war? Why did the original Mk VII family then stay in production for so long? Why did it take four long years to get the Mk X ready for production? But the fact is that after about 1954 the Mk VII/VIIM family was no longer a major player in Jaguar's strategy. In the 1950s and 1960s Jaguar was doing so much more than merely developing the occasional new model. Indeed, there were so many interlinked activities in this fast-growing concern that it is a miracle that the company was able to do so much with such limited resources. This chapter, therefore, is an attempt to tell a more complete story and to summarize how the company and its products changed in that period.

Given that I worked at Jaguar for some years during this period, I think I can understand some of the pressures which bore down on the company at the time. Even then, it was surprising to see such a compact business tackling so many different projects.

The management team was tiny and as the top man, Lyons took most of the decisions himself. With working capital always being limited there seemed to be a constant struggle to squeeze more production out of factory buildings which were not really equipped to deliver the goods. So how could such a small design team achieve so much, when even by the late 1950s there were fewer than forty drawing boards at Browns Lane? How could there ever have been the time and resources to build a professional 'works' racing team? And how was it that Jaguar could stay independent, and financially self-sufficient, until the mid-1960s?

BIGGER FACTORIES, FASTER CARS AND MORE MODELS

In 1945 William Lyons's master-plan – to develop an entirely new family of Jaguar cars in double-quick time – looked extremely ambitious, if not impossible. It was only his burning ambition and the belief in his vision of Jaguar's future, which brought it about at all. Faced with all the difficulties that surrounded him and given the suppliers he had, a lesser man might have backed down – but Lyons never seems to have hesitated. He was, above all, a practical man, so when faced with delays he had to let the renewal programme slip back a little.

Only those of us who lived through that

The 3½-litre saloon, styled and designed in the 1930s, still looked elegant in the late 1940s, when British buyers were still queueing up to buy one. The sweeping wing lines and the sinuous rear quarters were all typical of the 'Lyons theme' of the period.

Sir William Lyons, Jaguar's founder, was his company's mainspring, major shareholder, stylist and strategist throughout his working life.

3½-litre 'Mk IV' models were nobly styled in the fashion of the late 1930s, with a battery of lamps and flowing wing lines. 'Easyclean' wheel covers helped owners to keep the long, low car looking immaculate.

In the 1930s, styling fashion dictated a long bonnet, a cabin with a relatively low roof, and a compact cabin – all of which was readily embraced by Sir William Lyons when shaping the 3½-litre. Although this shape was similar to the original SS-Jaguars of 1935, the detail and construction were very different.

Drophead coupés were the rarest of the Mk Vs, this duotone colour scheme probably not being 'ex-works'. Note the characteristic external hood frame bars.

The Mk V of 1948 neatly spanned the pre-war style of the 'Mk IV' and the modern chassis and suspension which would also be used in the Mk VII. Larger, more capacious, and somewhat sleeker than the 'Mk IV' which it displaced, the Mk V was a capable and elegant Jaguar saloon.

Attention to detail. There is not a line out of place on the tail of the Mk V, which reflects the time William Lyons spent perfecting the design at the styling stage. Note that although there was no badging this car was still instantly recognizable.

The 3½-litre ohv engine of the 'Mk IV' and (here) the Mk V was a powerful and impressive unit, but not at all easy to service and repair.

Mk V drophead coupés used the same rear styling as the saloons, but aft of the windscreen their construction was very different. Two doors instead of four, and a complex fold-down soft-top all saw to that. Naturally the rear wheel spats could be removed for wheel changing and for attention to the back axle.

The Mk V facia / instrument panel, with all instruments mounted on wood. The large wheel was necessary to keep steering efforts down to an acceptable level. Pity about the 'umbrella-handle' handbrake though, which was mounted ahead of the (UK) driver's right knee.

Third in a long-running family, the Mk VIII's styling was virtually the same as that of the ousted Mk VIIM. Except for the use of a one-piece windscreen, the front-end aspect was the same. This owner is sharing his one-make club allegiances as fairly as possible!

As there was no question of making sheet-metal style changes when moving from Mk VIIM to Mk VIII, Sir William devoted time and attention to getting the duotone treatment exactly right. Controversial at the time, there was no doubt that it helped to break up the expanse of flanks, making the latest car look slightly sleeker than before.

464 HYV, now part of Jaguar's own collection, is probably the most notable Mk VII type of all. Having started life as a Mk VIIM in the mid 1950s, it was delivered to Her Majesty the Queen Mother and was then regularly updated in the following years, effectively becoming a Mk IX, complete with disc brakes and the later version of the radiator grille.

The unique Mk VIIM/MkIX, as owned by Her Majesty the Queen Mother for many years, shows off the rounded but (for Vintage 1950) amazingly sleek lines which Williams Lyons and Fred Gardner's craftsmen had evolved. It is difficult to realize that all these cars had a 120in (3,048mm) wheelbase or that their top speeds were all comfortably over 100mph (160km/h).

By 1960 this particular shape of 'Big Jaguar' was nearing the end of its ten-year career. This particular Mk X was built in 1960 and shows off one of the many duotone colour schemes made available on later models.

Wider, longer and with a bigger cabin than the old Mk IX, the Mk X was the largest Jaguar ever to be put on sale. Launched in 1961, this monocoque would be built until 1970, when the era of truly 'Big Jaguars' came to an end.

The Mk X gave way to the 420G (this particular car) in 1966, though even a Jaguar fanatic had to look very closely to pick out the differences. The 420G, in fact, was always distinguished by the slim chrome strip along the flanks – the Mk X never had that feature.

From this three-quarter rear angle, the Mk X/420G style has many visual links with the smaller S-type/420 Jaguars, including the small but definite rear wing extensions to support the tail lamps, the wide and low stance, and the characteristic rear windows and three-quarter window lines. In fact the Mk X/420G boot was very large, but rather shallow.

time know how war-weary Britain and its inhabitants had really become by 1945. Behind all the flag-waving and the patriotic cinema newsreel stories, the truth was less uplifting. When the fighting finally stopped in August 1945, millions of men and women could not immediately stop, stand back, smile with relief and get on with their lives once again. It was going to takes months, years perhaps, for the nightmare to recede. A way of life – that of the 1930s – had been shattered and would never return. So, too, were the cities and the factories which had suffered so much. It wasn't merely that six years of fighting had seen so many buildings destroyed, and that so many fine people had been killed, but that the carnage had broken so many spirits, while personal tragedies made continuing life so unbearable for many.

First of all, therefore, Jaguar had to rebuild itself, reassemble its staff and only then could it start building new products. Once the last of the 1940-model cars had been assembled, the Foleshill factory had been turned over completely to war work. Naturally a large number of motorcycle side-cars had been produced, along with thousands of trailers, but by 1945 the emphasis was on construction and repair of large fuselage sections for fighting aircraft, notably the Whitley and Stirling bombers (early on), and the Spitfire, Mosquito and Meteor fighter planes.

Although the centre of Coventry had been devastated by bombing in November 1940, amazingly, there was very little bomb damage to Jaguar's own factories. Except on one occasion, when the most modern of its buildings had lost its roof in an incendiary attack, the biggest problems were when power supplies failed and in getting staff to and from the site over rubble-strewn roads.

Every car-maker found that it took a great deal longer than hoped to re-convert its buildings to peace-time production. For Jaguar the upheaval was made more difficult because of Lyons's purchase (from Standard) of all the machine tools and fixtures needed to manufacture six-cylinder engines.

Although the European war officially ended on 8 May 1945, and the Japanese surrender followed on 15 August, Jaguar did not complete its first post-war private car – a 1½-litre saloon – until September. Even so, post-war production had been previewed in July 1945, when Lyons told the press that in the next two years: '... exports alone will exceed the total pre-war production for any similar period ...', but the first six-cylinder cars were not actually delivered until January 1946.

Even then, the build up of deliveries was slow, so that in the first post-war year, which ended on 31 July 1946, a mere 1,132 cars were delivered. Certainly this was not due to any lack of orders – there was actually a colossal demand for any new car at this stage – but to the difficulty in getting deliveries of parts.

For the next three years, Jaguar and every other British car-maker struggled to get back to pre-war levels of production, in a threateningly hostile economic climate. With Britain's reserves long since exhausted by the cost of waging war, the country was deeply in debt to the USA. One consequence was that the government demanded high export quotas from all manufacturers, so that every effort would be made to raise hard currency to pay off those debts.

Coincidentally, there was a shortage of sheet steel capacity in the UK at the time, so to impose such quotas on sometimes reluctant manufacturers, the government would only allocate sheet steel supplies to those who agreed to fall in line. Jaguar, with very little export success behind it, had no choice but to comply, as this summary of deliveries proves:

Financial year	Total production	Cars exported	Export percentage
1937/8	2,209	188	8.5
1938/9	5,378	252	4.7
1939/40	899	82	9.1

the War then intervened:

1945/6	1,132	316	27.9
1946/7	4,342	949	41.2
1947/8	4,184	2,173	51.9

Incidentally, this rapid recovery was achieved in spite of Britain being hit by the worst winter on record in 1947, and by drastic shortages of energy – coal supplies, oil and electricity in particular – which hit the country so hard that factories were actually forced to close down for a period.

BUILDING THE BODIES

Having started life as a specialist coach-builder (Swallow), Jaguar was naturally reluctant to give up that part of its heritage. In twenty years, however, the business had changed so much, along with a revolution in styling and construction, that it became inevitable.

When SS was building only fifty cars a week, it was still possible for them to have traditional bodies, made by covering wooden skeletons with steel panels, and the company was expert at this. When SS-Jaguar aimed to build 100 saloon cars a week it made more economic sense to build all-steel shells, but more pressings were needed and the company had to engage outside suppliers to provide them.

Now, in the post-war years, Lyons wanted to see Jaguar build more cars than ever before. However, it was soon clear that his relatively simply equipped business would not be able to build all the bodies for those

Pressed Steel Co. Ltd

Starting with the Mk VII model, Jaguar then sourced all its saloon car bodyshells – whether separate or unit-construction types, from the Pressed Steel Co. Ltd of Cowley, near Oxford.

Originally founded in 1926 as a joint venture between Morris Motors and the Edward G. Budd Manufacturing Co. of the USA, Pressed Steel specialized in building welded-together all-steel bodies, all its initial supplies going to Morris. However, because of its obvious financial and geographical links with Morris, Pressed Steel found it difficult to gain orders from other car-makers, the result being that Morris pragmatically sold out its shareholding in 1930. Thereafter Pressed Steel expanded rapidly, and by the end of the 1930s it was doing business with every member of the British 'Big Six' car-makers.

SS Cars, later Jaguar Cars, originally took some pressings towards building its own 1½/2½/3½-litre and Mk V saloon shells, but for the projected Mk VII it was decided to source the entire shell, still in what the industry quaintly called the 'Body in White' (unpainted) state, from a specialist.

Only two independent companies – Pressed Steel and Fisher & Ludlow of Birmingham – were large enough to cope with Jaguar's requirements, so Pressed Steel (already known to Jaguar) got the business. Mk VII shells were soon joined by monocoque 2.4/3.4-litre shells, and the largest Jaguar of all, the Mk X, took over in 1961.

By this time Pressed Steel was very large indeed, for in addition to Jaguar it was also supplying BMC, Rootes, Rolls-Royce, Rover, Standard-Triumph and Daimler with shells. When it was taken over by BMC in 1965 Jaguar had doubts about their security of future supplies, but after Jaguar joined forces with BMC that concern evaporated.

After the foundation of British Leyland, Pressed Steel became subsumed into Pressed Steel Fisher, but Jaguar continued to take bodyshell supplies for many years until it developed its own body plant at Castle Bromwich in the 1980s.

cars. Accordingly, he approached Pressed Steel, Britain's largest independent bodyshell constructor, to become his new supplier.

As already described in an earlier chapter, Jaguar was just one of many firms which was hammering on Pressed Steel's doors, demanding service and priority over its rivals. Unhappily for Jaguar, though, as a new customer it had to stand in line behind Pressed Steel's long-established customers, who also happened to place a lot more business in that direction.

With the exception of Rolls-Royce, whose new Bentley-badged 'standard steel' bodyshell was actually previewed early in 1946, no other Pressed Steel customer got their hands on newly-designed shells until 1948. Looking at the Earls Court Motor Show line up of new Pressed Steel-built shells in October of that year – which included the Hillman Minx, Humber Hawk,

Morris Oxford, Morris Six, Rover 75 P3, Wolseley 4/50 and Wolseley 6/80 models – it was quite easy to see why Jaguar could not immediately persuade Pressed Steel to tool-up for the building of a new large Jaguar saloon. Nor was there space in the year which followed, as Rover required a new P4 shell at the end of 1949. This explains why Jaguar was obliged to assemble its own Mk V shells (and why those assembly numbers were relatively restricted) and it also explains why complete Pressed Steel-built Mk VII shells could not be readied until the autumn of 1950.

Although Mk VII production was actually a simpler operation than the Mk V had been, there was still a difficult and complex jig-saw to be completed every time a car was assembled. Since the saloon car shell no longer had to be welded-up from individual sections, nor was there a drop-head coupé alternative to be considered, Jaguar actually

Jaguar styles separated by forty years, the Mk V having been assembled at the Foleshill factory, while the 1994/5 model XJ6 was assembled at Browns Lane.

found itself at first with a little more bodyshop space at Foleshill, though this was soon taken up with the assembly of more XK120s.

Although Jaguar machined and assembled all of its own engines and gearboxes, much of the rest of the Mk VII was bought-in from specialist suppliers. Rubery Owen provided chassis frames, rear axles were by ENV or Salisbury, Girling provided brakes, Lucas all the electrical fittings, Smiths the instruments, Wilmot Breeden all the bumpers and brightwork, Triplex the glass and Dunlop the tyres. Not only that, but overdrives came from Laycock and automatic transmissions from Borg Warner.

Dampers might be in one truck, springs on another and steering gear on the next. Then, as later, Jaguar was more of an assembler than a manufacturer, for fighting their way through those trucks were vehicles from Connolly, which provided the leather, along with specialists who delivered wood and carpets for Jaguar to shape and form its own trim.

FROM FOLESHILL TO BROWNS LANE

As we now know, if Lyons had gained permission to erect new factory buildings to the

This aerial shot of the original Browns Lane complex, probably taken during the war in the 1940s when the growth of housing in Allesley still had to follow, shows the original 'shadow factory' layout. What became Jaguar's administrative offices (close to the Browns Lane frontage) are towards the centre right of this shot.

west of the existing Foleshill site, Jaguar might never have moved to Browns Lane in 1951/1952. Even so, with the existing Foleshill plant already bursting at the seams, one brief look at these important Jaguar dates shows that some sort of move was inevitable:

1945   Purchase of existing six-cylinder engine-making plant from Standard Motor Co. Ltd
1946/7   4,342 cars built – almost back up to pre-war levels
1948   Introduction of new Mk V saloon and XK120 sports car
1949/50   Re-launch of the XK120 as a series-production sports car Introduction of the Mk VII saloon 6,647 cars produced in twelve months – a new Jaguar record
[1951/2   Move to a new factory at Browns Lane, Allesley]
1951   Start-up of major racing programme Introduction of the C-Type
1952   Limited production of C-Types began
1952/3   10,114 cars produced in twelve months – yet another record
1954   The XK140 took over from the XK120 Limited-production of the D-Type authorized
1955   More massive expansion – with introduction of the third model line – the compact, monocoque, 2.4-litre model
1955/6   Yet another record production year – 12,152 cars

Looking back, it almost seems impossible for Jaguar to have fitted in as much as they actually did – and if Lyons had refused to get involved in motor racing one could certainly see why!

In this first post-war decade Jaguar's

image blossomed all round the world. Not only did the XK-engined cars become more and more popular world-wide, but the business provided more and more employment in Coventry, which was booming once again. Jaguar's after-tax profits soared from £1,413 in 1945, to £159,198 in 1950, and on again to £260,343 in 1955.

As Jaguar authority Andrew Whyte once wrote:

> Recognition of his remarkable achievements, particularly in building the export business and the company itself, came to Lyons in the 1956 New Year's Honours List, when he was made a Knight Bachelor.

To every Jaguar enthusiast and watcher, the only surprise was that this had been such a long time in coming. Thereafter, Jaguar's founder would be known as Sir William, a title which always sat more comfortably on his immaculately clad shoulders than, merely, 'Mr Lyons'.

FIRE, NEAR-DISASTER AND SPEEDY RECOVERY

Only one year after H.M. The Queen had honoured Jaguar, not only by knighting its chairman, but by paying an official visit to the Browns Lane plant to inspect the latest production cars and the 'works' D-Type race cars, Jaguar looked set for further expansion, its morale at a new high. Yet another victory at Le Mans – the fourth in six years – had confirmed the excellence of the XK engine, though Jaguar then felt obliged to withdraw from motorsport while it was still at the peak.

Technically there seemed to be new Jaguar models all around. Early in 1957 the road-going XKSS had just been shown, the Mk VIII had gone on sale, the 3.4-litre model was due for launch and the XK150 was soon

Before the massive expansion at Browns Lane began, there were two models in production – the Mk VII and the XK120 models – and parallel Trim Tracks could deal with either model, as this picture makes clear.

due to take over from the XK140. Not only that, but design work was well-advanced on a V12 engine, and the first of the excitingly styled E-Types was being made.

Unhappily, therefore, it was time for fate – and near-tragedy – to step in. On Tuesday, 12 February 1957, after many of the workforce had gone home for the evening, fire broke out in the production line stores at the northern end of the Browns Lane factory, spreading rapidly and consuming one third of the floor space, including the new-car despatch bay and the last remaining stock of D-Type race cars.

Writing in *The Motor* a few days later, Midland Editor Harold Hastings wrote that:

Sir William Lyons, the chairman and managing director, was directing the fire brigade to a link road which partially separates the main block and forms a natural fire break ...

Frank Raymond Wilton ('Lofty') England

Although 'Lofty' – few other than Sir William Lyons ever called him anything else! – is more famous as Jaguar's motorsport team manager, he was also an important executive at Jaguar through the 'Big Jaguar' years. When the 3½-litre was at its height he was the company's service manager, and by the time the last 420G of all was produced, he had become Jaguar's joint managing director.

Born and educated in London, 'Lofty' was then apprenticed to Daimler's depot in Hendon, as an engineer, where his nickname was soon a recognition of his tall figure. This was after having become a racing mechanic to, among others, Sir Henry 'Tim' Birkin, Whitney Straight, Dick Seaman and Prince Birabongse Bhanuban ('B. Bira').

Having joined Alvis, of Coventry, as a service engineer, and serving as a Lancaster pilot with the RAF during the Second World War, he became Jaguar's service manager in 1946. During the 1950s he combined this job with that of competitions manager, presiding over victories at Le Mans in 1951, 1953 and 1955.

From 1956 'Lofty' became service director and had to withdraw from active involvement in motorsport, for he then began to move inexorably up the management ladder. In 1961 (the year in which the Mk X was introduced) he became assistant managing director, in 1966 he was appointed deputy managing director (the year in which Jaguar joined hands with BMC), then in 1967 Sir William Lyons made him his joint managing director, a position he retained for years after Jaguar was subsumed into British Leyland.

Throughout the 1950s and 1960s, therefore, 'Lofty' was a party to every decision made regarding the Big Jaguars. When Sir William stepped down in 1972, he then became Jaguar's chief executive, but held this position for less than two years, before retiring.

Along with his second wife, he soon moved to a retirement home in Austria. Although that was the end of his active involvement in business, he remained fiercely loyal to Jaguar, its image and its heritage. Though living far from Great Britain, he kept closely in touch with every motoring development. Motoring writers like myself soon learned to check and double check all Jaguar material written, for woe-betide any of us who made mistakes – the admonitory letter would soon arrive!

Sadly, Lofty died in 1995.

Meanwhile, staff were making frantic efforts to save as many of the cars in the packed dispatch bay as possible. Racing driver Bob Berry was dashing back and forth and gave up only when he was ordered to desist as he drove out one model with the roof lining burning over his head.

Service Director F.R.W. ('Lofty') England was organizing a rescue party in the service department, preserving cars and records ...

When I finally left, the directors were already discussing measures to restart production [author's emphasis]. But a quarter of the million square feet of floor area in the main building had been gutted, and a third damaged.

Although management and workmen managed to save 300 cars – more than a week's production – by pushing or driving them to safety, the immediate cost, estimated at £3,500,000, was horrendous. At first it looked as if the factory would have to be idle for weeks, perhaps even months, but a breeze-block wall was immediately thrown up to seal off the undamaged buildings, after which the rebuilding could get started.

Since no damage had been done to paint, trim, engine assembly and machine shops – or to the separate office, design and experimental departments – the business, as a business, was still intact, though a good deal of work was needed to get the three main models – Mk VIII, 2.4-litre and XK140 – back into production.

Within two days some order was beginning to return out of chaos, as Hastings reported:

Elsewhere, whilst fork-lift trucks and breakdown wagons were lifting and dragging the last of the 200 [the final figure was actually 270] fire-ravaged cars out to an enormous temporary graveyard in front of the main executive building, other men were working on a shortened finishing line. The first results of their efforts left the factory for delivery by mid-day, 36 hours after the fire.

In his office in the separate executive block, Sir William Lyons explained his plans. The first job, he said, was to complete the 300 nearly finished models which had been saved, and to start a shortened assembly line which would be gradually extended as the gutted part of the building was being rebuilt.

In two or three weeks' time, completely post-fire models will be coming off the shortened lines, the production gathering momentum week by week.

As I congratulated Sir William on these wonderful efforts on leaving, his last words to me were: 'We'll do the job all right – the fire makes it a little harder, that's all'.

Rival manufacturers and suppliers (Dunlop, noticeably) offered help, storage space and other facilities, which were rapidly taken up, but 'ghouls' looking for cheap, fire-damaged Jaguars were speedily dismissed. Within ten days Jaguar announced that hundreds of offers had been turned away:

Not only are bodies being cut up, piecemeal, with oxy-acetylene cutters, but engines, gearboxes, axles, springs and other components are being cut through and then hammered into a condition rendering them useless for anything but scrap.

Pictures show that many of the cars lost in this fire were Mk VIII models, but the record also shows that Jaguar made a remarkable recovery from this trauma. The workforce, put on part-time working for a few weeks (there was simply not enough space to accommodate them on the shortened lines for a while), was soon back in full swing.

For Lyons, his staff and all the dealers, the heartening news was that there seemed to be no loss of custom, and the waiting lists caused by the fiery hiatus were cheerfully accepted.

The ruined section of the factory was speedily chopped down, bulldozed into heaps and cleared away. Four weeks after the fire, work began on a new extension, and only sixteen weeks after the fire had broken out a new 80,000sq ft (7,500sq m) area was virtually ready for use. Even so, when I first visited the factory as a graduate employee in September 1957, temporary expedients were all around and normality would not be restored for several further months.

Once the new buildings had been shaken down, Jaguar production rose to more than 300, sometimes up to nearly 400, every week, and since every staffman's earnings included a production-bonus element there was always great interest in the published figures which were placarded at the end of the finishing lines!

Amazingly, in spite of the fire, and the disruption it caused to assembly, to the stocking of parts, and to the efficient running of the business, more cars were built in the twelve-month period including the fire than ever before – 800 more cars than in the previous year.

The big leap forward, however, followed in the next two years. Not only did the Mk VIII continue to sell very well, as did the XK150 sports car, but more and more people queued up to purchase the monocoque 2.4-litre and 3.4-litre cars. By mid-1959 up to 500 cars a week were flooding out of Browns Lane, the total achievement for the 1958/9 financial year being 20,876.

BUILDING AN EMPIRE

In the early 1960s, a lesser man than Sir William Lyons might have neglected his core business, or delegated more to his subordinates, for this was the period in which the business expanded enormously. In less than five years several sizeable businesses, with famous names and histories, were added to the Jaguar 'empire', the implications for the marque's future being enormous.

Jaguar, remember, had been totally independent since 1945, when it bought back the six-cylinder engine-making capability from the Standard Motor Co. Ltd, though like other independents it was still heavily dependent on companies like Pressed Steel, Lucas, Dunlop, Smiths and Wilmot Breeden for many of its components.

By the end of the 1950s, however, it was once again running out of space. Browns Lane, so much larger and more promising than Foleshill when originally taken over in 1952, was now bursting at the seams, for Jaguar had quadrupled its sales and production in less than ten years.

With the Mk2 range just put on sale (and every sign that demand was set to rise still further) and with the development of the new E-Type and Mk X models well under way, it was clear that more factory space was needed – and fast.

Like every other British motor industry tycoon of the period, Lyons was thoroughly disillusioned by government restrictions on business expansion. In a misguided effort to shore-up decaying areas of Britain ('development areas', as they were called), and to inject modern technologies into regions used only to building ships or digging for coal, Coventry-based companies wanting to expand in Coventry were brusquely told that this would not be allowed.

ACQUISITION OF DAIMLER

Sir William dutifully inspected various sites but found them all wanting. For a time, the impasse was unbreakable, until word got round that the Coventry-based Daimler business might be for sale. For the second time in less than a decade, here was the chance to make a deal with Daimler – the first having been the annexation of Browns Lane in 1951/2.

Not only did Daimler have a large factory just to the north of Coventry's city centre, but there was spare capacity as it was actually under-used. Even though buying the Daimler business was going to cost a lot of money – the final purchase price was £3,400,000 – this seemed to be an irresistible deal. Not only was 'The Daimler' plant close to Jaguar – it was three miles away – but it was too large for Daimler's existing activities and there were exciting possibilities in the bus and military vehicle sectors which would also come with the purchase.

Immediately after Jaguar took over Daimler in June 1960, the company stated:

> Jaguar Cars Ltd wish to deny unfounded rumours to the effect that sweeping changes including even the extinction of the Daimler marque, are to be expected. Whilst one of the most obvious and immediate benefits accruing to Jaguar as a result of their purchase is the availability of much-needed additional production facilities for Jaguar cars, the Company's long term view envisages not merely the retention of the Daimler marque, but the expansion of its markets at home and overseas.

This was a masterpiece of PR-speak, which actually revealed very little. It was true that

137

Compared with the view on page 132, this 1980s study of Browns Lane shows just how many extra buildings and how much extra capacity had been squeezed out of the site. The original administrative offices, somewhat modified, are on the centre right of this shot. More changes would follow in the 1990s when a new bypass road was constructed roughly on the left margin of this picture.

When Jaguar took over Daimler in 1960, it inherited a large and somewhat under-utilized factory. This was Daimler's Radford plant in the 1980s, considerably redeveloped and modernized, but still old-fashioned enough to horrify Ford managers when they took over the business in 1989. Jaguar chose the major building to the right (the east, in fact) of the central factory driveway to manufacture engines and transmissions, the V12 and AJ6/AJ16 transfer lines being installed there in the 1970s and 1980s. The block at the top of the picture was not part of the Daimler purchase, for Standard-Triumph had taken it over for transmission assembly purposes in the late 1950s.

The Daimler Purchase

When Sir William Lyons announced the takeover of Daimler in 1960, it caused a sensation, for there had been no rumours ahead of the breaking of the news.

Daimler had started building cars in Coventry in 1896, using German designs, and was purchased by the BSA (Birmingham Small Arms) company in 1910. Along the way Daimler attracted royal patronage which was retained until the 1950s. BSA also rescued Lanchester from bankruptcy in 1931, this combine then prospering in Coventry at the Radford factory, where it built cars, public service buses and coaches and – from 1939 – military vehicles.

Needing extra factory space for expansion (with which Daimler was well-provided), Sir William Lyons approached BSA, who sold the Daimler/Lanchester business to him for £3.4 million in June 1960. At the same time Sir William insisted that he intended to expand Jaguar and Daimler, a promise which he certainly kept.

Assembly of 'Daimler' models was wound down during the 1960s, after which a series of 'badge-engineered' 'Daimler-Jaguar' models took over. At the same time, Jaguar's engine and gearbox manufacturing facilities were moved into Daimler's Radford factory, where they stayed into the 1990s. Both the V12 and the modern-generation AJ6 engines were manufactured on this site.

Daimler, as a marque name, is still a prominent part of the Jaguar model line, though public transport and military vehicle activity was abandoned some years ago. The Radford factory, progressively modernized, is still an important part of Jaguar's Coventry operations.

Jaguar had bought Daimler, intending to retain the badge and to expand its influence, and it was also true that Jaguar needed the 'additional production facilities', but how this was to be done was another matter.

Lyons, in fact, well knew that Jaguar could sell many more cars if only it could build more of them. Browns Lane, on the other hand, had virtually reached its limit. Now, following the Daimler purchase, it made no long-term sense to carry on painting, trimming and assembling cars on two sites – Browns Lane and Radford – or to carry on with two large, unconnected, machine shop facilities.

In mid-1960 two other major manufacturing headaches were already becoming evident. One was that the last of the 'separate chassis' Jaguars – the XK150 and the Mk IX models – would be built in 1961. Traditionally, Jaguar had always assembled its own sports car bodies from panels or sub-assemblies, and this process was due to continue with the E-Type, a monocoque shell which was certain to take more time to assemble than the XK150 ever had.

Both these forthcoming events meant that manufacture at Browns Lane would need to be much modified. More space would be needed for sports car bodyshell manufacture, and the assembly lines previously given over to manufacture of the separate-chassis cars would have to be modified to deal with monocoque cars instead – as an example, the engine/gearbox assemblies would have to arrive at a different point in the sequence and from a different angle.

In a bold and ambitious strategy, therefore, speedily set in motion in 1960, Jaguar's production experts, led by Jack Silver, started a major reorganization. Although this was going to take years to achieve, the intention was to turn Browns Lane into the final assembly factory for cars, while Radford would carry on assembling military and public service vehicles. All Jaguar's machining, plus the engine and transmission manufacturing departments, would be relocated at Radford.

In the short term, it was inevitable that assembly of Daimler cars would continue at Radford and that Daimler's machining capability would have to shuffle up to make space for Jaguar facilities to move in, but in the end this was achieved.

In fact Daimler's non-car assembly business persisted until the early 1970s (when the space was taken up by brand-new machinery for making Jaguar V12 engines). The first 'Daimler-Jaguar' models (the V8 engined 2½-litre saloon and 420-based Sovereign) were always built at Browns Lane, but the old-type Daimlers carried on at Radford until the end – the Majestic until 1962, the SP250 until 1964, the Majestic Major and DR450 Limousine models until 1968.

Even today, many Jaguar enthusiasts still do not realize how much change and modernization was achieved at Browns Lane in the early 1960s. This revolution allowed a complete re-jig of the layout, and more than half the space of all the operation found itself in a different place when the reorganization was finally completed. Elderly machine tools, bought for the Second World War effort in the early 1940s and originally bolted down in Foleshill, found themselves being moved yet again, and a fleet of contractors' lorries were kept very busy for years to come!

When the engine build, transmission build and large machine shops had been moved to Radford, trim shops once squeezed into another corner of Browns Lane took their place. The alignment of final assembly, trim and finishing lines was revolutionized. A new (to Jaguar!) body-finishing and paint plant was installed – this having been bought from Mulliners in Birmingham, disassembled, then re-erected at Browns Lane.

Not only that, but Jaguar finally got the chance to buy what had become known as the 'GEC' office building at the south-western extremity of the original shadow factory site. Not available when Jaguar came to occupy Browns Lane in 1961/62, this 150,000sq ft (14,000sq m) complex was finally annexed in 1961 and speedily converted to house all Jaguar's design, engineering, test

and development departments.

At a stroke this also released space in the original office complex on the north-west front and finally allowed dispersed experimental and test facilities to be brought together. It was a signal, too, for various smaller, subsidiary buildings around the main under-one-roof factory to be rationalized and expanded. By the 1970s, indeed, aerial views showed Browns Lane to be a much more complex site than it had been in the early 1950s. All in all, these changes made it easier, faster and more profitable to build cars at Browns Lane: in spite of the heavy investment in new models, profits moved up from £1.02 million in 1960 to £1.66 million in 1965.

However, although the old-design, separate-chassis, Mk IX gave way to the larger, more modern, but heavier monocoque Mk X in 1961/2, even more important changes were brewing at Jaguar. These could only be tackled when the corporate jig-saw had settled down yet again. Not only was work proceeding on even further enlarged versions of the XK engine – upping the capacity from 3,781 to 4,235cc was much more complex than it sounds, for merely wielding the cylinder boring bar was not enough – but it was finally time to replace the old Moss-type gearbox with an all-new all-synchromesh design.

FURTHER TAKEOVERS

In the meantime, Sir William Lyons was taking further steps to expand his empire. First, in October 1961, he bought the Guy Motors business (of Wolverhampton) from the Receiver. Guy, a long-established Wolverhampton builder of commercial vehicles, was partly aligned with Daimler in the years which followed.

Next, in March 1963, he took over Coventry-Climax of Coventry, a company which produced not only world-famous Formula One race engines, but also less complex engines and fork-lift trucks for many other markets. One of the 'assets' of the business was its technical director, Walter Hassan, who was soon given a dual responsibility, that of looking after the development of Jaguar engines for the future. His work on Coventry-Climax racing engines soon dwindled, but development of Jaguar's brand new V12 unit then came on apace.

Like Jaguar, Coventry-Climax had been controlled by one man – Leonard Lee – for many years, but he was now looking to retire and found Jaguar an ideal 'home' for the family business. Coincidentally, but with no great commercial significance, Coventry-Climax's factory was but a few hundred yards from that of the Jaguar (ex-Daimler) Radford premises, and for years there was still no Jaguar 'evidence' there.

Finally, in the winter of 1964/5, Jaguar not only set up links with Cummins Engine Co. Inc., of Indiana, USA (the object being to manufacture engines in the UK to use in Guy and Daimler commercial vehicles), but there also came the chance to buy Henry Meadows, another Wolverhampton concern which just happened to be next door to the

Browns Lane in the 1990s looked sprucer than ever before, but still used most of the original buildings. A shot taken to show off several ages of Jaguar – SS100, Mk V and modern XJ6 and XJS models all feature – also details the frontage of the administrative offices which were built by Jaguar in the 1950s.

Mk X and Mk2 assembly at the Browns Lane factory in the early 1960s. This factory had continuously been upgraded and expanded during Jaguar's first decade of tenure – especially after the near-disastrous fire of 1957.

Guy business. By then Meadows, once a respected proprietary supplier of car engines to companies like Lagonda and Invicta, was a truck engine builder, and the Cummins engines might well have been built there. This, however, was a step too far in Jaguar's strategies, for the Cummins engines were not suitable, so the agreement was dissolved and the Guy site sold off.

Through and around all this, Mk X assembly continued undisturbed. Reconstruction at Browns Lane was largely completed by the time the Mk X went on sale at the end of 1961, and when the time came for Radford to start delivering the 4.2-litre engines and the all-synchromesh gearboxes, the Mk X was one of the very first 'customers' for those units.

Family likeness? Jaguar's S-Type was really a much modified Mk II, using Mk X-style independent rear suspension and a new tail-end style rather like that of the Mk X. This was all so typical of the way Jaguar's operations ballooned during the 1960s.

Merging with BMC

After Sir William Lyons's only son, John, was killed in a road accident in France (in a Mk VII) in 1955, there was no obvious family way that Jaguar's founder could hand on his family-owned business when he came to retire.

For years no one dared even raise the subject in his presence, but finally in 1966, when he was nearly 65 years old, Sir William Lyons suddenly announced his intention of merging the Jaguar Group (which already included Daimler-Lanchester, Coventry-Climax, Henry Meadows and Guy Motors), with the British Motor Corporation. This was Britain's largest car-making group, and included Austin, Morris, MG, Riley and Wolseley.

By 1965 Jaguar had been approached regarding mergers by several larger firms, notably Leyland Motors, but the approach from Sir George Harriman, BMC's chairman, was the first which seemed to offer him autonomy. Since BMC had already bought up Pressed Steel, this also offered him a secure tenure of body supplies.

A coincident approach by Leyland to both companies was turned down as being too complex to lay out and the agreed merger between Jaguar and BMC was made public on 29 July 1966. A new holding company, British Motor Holdings (BMH), was created to look after both groups.

Sir William remained as Jaguar's chairman and chief executive, his freedom of operation unrestricted. At the same time he became a director of BMH. With the exceptions that BMC soon dropped a few unprofitable models and began to distribute Jaguars in certain export territories, the coming together was very limited indeed.

BMH only lasted until the spring of 1968, when it was submerged into the new British Leyland combine.

PRESSED STEEL, BMC AND LEYLAND

By the mid-1960s one of Jaguar's longest-standing supply arrangements was that there should be smooth, regular and untroubled delivery of Mk X bodyshells from Pressed Steel to Browns Lane. In July 1965, therefore, imagine Lyons's surprise and consternation when BMC suddenly announced that it was to take over Pressed Steel!

Although BMC promptly announced that it intended '... to maintain the existing goodwill and business relations that Pressed Steel enjoy with their own customers', shrewd industrial writers pointed out that Jaguar, Rover, Rolls-Royce, Standard-Triumph and the Rootes Group all used Pressed Steel and could no longer rely on this company, long-term, for future supplies.

The outcome was predictable. Standard-Triumph and Rootes began to build up their own in-house supplies, Rover dashed for safety under Leyland's wing, while Sir William Lyons seriously began to ponder his future.

In many ways, though, Lyons was not ready to plan Jaguar's future. In 1965 he was still only sixty-four years of age, remarkably vigorous and forward-looking, and still look forward to years of managerial control. This was just as well. The Lyons family still held financial control over Jaguar, but because his son John had been killed in a road accident on the way to Le Mans in the 1950s there was no family successor to the founder.

Every other firm in Britain's motor industry realized this, which meant that Lyons was never short of merger offers, all of which were politely refused. Then, in mid-1966, and strictly on his own terms, he

Into British Leyland

Although Leyland did not merge with BMH (which included the Jaguar Group) until 1968, takeover or merger talks had been simmering for some years before that.

Leyland, which absorbed Standard-Triumph in 1961, then Rover (including Alvis) in 1966, had talked generally to Jaguar several times during the 1960s, and made the first approach to BMC in 1964. Leyland thought it was close to forging a tripartite agreement with BMC and Jaguar in 1966, but was finally rebuffed, and the BMH merger went on without Leyland's involvement.

Talks with BMH (originally regarding joint overseas projects) were re-opened in 1967, but it was not until the autumn that a genuine, full-scale merger was discussed, with the Government's blessing. Through all these talks Sir William Lyons was anxious to stress that he wanted Jaguar to retain its autonomy (freedom of independent operation) but was otherwise happy to support a merger.

The final terms were thrashed out in January 1968, the merger proposal was made public on 17 January, and after every commercial wrinkle had been squeezed out of the deal, Jaguar became just one element of the massive British Leyland Motor Corporation. Sir William Lyons remained as Chairman of Jaguar, but also became a director of BLMC.

Although Jaguar retained its virtual independence until the late 1970s (when Rover gearboxes came to be used in Jaguar XJ saloons for the first time), there was a constant battle to maintain company morale. It would not truly be restored again until the company was privatized in 1984.

finally agreed for Jaguar to join forces with the BMC combine. The result was a new holding company, British Motor Holdings (BMH), and although Lyons immediately became a director of BMH, there was never any direct BMC influence on Jaguar's policies, which was a condition he had always placed on the deal.

For the Mk X, which was about to turn into the 420G, this underpinned the future for its body supplies, as Pressed Steel could now be considered as 'family'. This, in any case, was just as well, as the Mk X/420G's successor, the XJ6, was ready for body tooling to be produced, and the only viable firm to undertake that work was Pressed Steel!

In the end, everything seemed to have worked out well. Everything, indeed, looked rosy for the next eighteen months, until BMH chose to join forces with Leyland. This, though placarded as an amicable merger, produced a rambling conglomerate which came to be dominated by Leyland. Slowly, painfully and unhappily, Jaguar tended to be submerged in Leyland's master plans, though the last of the 420Gs was built before the situation became critical. In particular, much of what Lyons had wanted to achieve with Daimler and Guy was overtaken by events. The Mk X/420G range, in fact, was developed, built and modified in Jaguar's most turbulent modern period, and the next chapter tells its story.

8 Mk X and 420G: the Biggest Jaguars of All

When it came to designing new cars, Sir William Lyons was used to moving quickly, but that strategy was not successful in the case of the Mk X project. First considered in 1958, but not finally shaped until 1960, and launched in 1961, it did not actually go on sale until 1962. This was the period in which I was working at Jaguar in the design and development departments. I was privileged to see some of the ways in which Sir William Lyons worked and to see why the Mk X took so long to arrive. Not many people are aware of the fact that the Mk VIII was originally meant to be the last of that particular separate-chassis line, and that the 'Zenith' project (as the new big monocoque model was

Late-1950s sketches from the Jaguar archive all show the way that the 'Zenith' (Mk X) front end might have looked.

coded) was originally due to take over as the 'new Mk IX'.

This, though, was before Sir William got involved in an urgent restyle for the 2.4-litre/3.4-litre models, evolving the Mk 2 models, and before the chance to buy Daimler came along. At the same time the E-Type was gradually (sometimes painfully) being converted from a race car to a road-going sports car. It was no wonder then, that cynical designers began to rename the proposed 'Mk Nine' as the 'Mk Time'.

In spite of the delays, and while Lyons and Fred Gardner kept beavering away at the development of a new style, Bill Heynes was able to give his design team a few basic dimensions to work around. In a classic case of working inwards from the tyre contact patches, Heynes told his staff to assume that a new Dunlop RS5 tyre of 7.50 x 14in would eventually be used, and that the now 'traditional' 120in (3,048mm) wheelbase would also be retained. Not, however, that this gave chassis designers like Tom Jones much to go on, for until the wheel tracks were also established (and it would be Lyons who finally settled those as part of the overall styling package) the suspension systems could not be detailed.

INTRODUCING THE MK X

Up in the design offices on the first floor of Browns Lane's main office block, top staff had an idea of what Sir William Lyons was trying to achieve with 'Zenith', but few were allowed to see his inspirational style until it was finalized. Although it was not actually 'mission impossible', Lyons had a very difficult job to do. 'Zenith' had to replace a car (the Mk VII family) whose design roots were in the 1940s, a car which had been technically advanced when new, but which had been overtaken by its rivals in recent years.

The major technical change now begging

to be made was for Jaguar to abandon the separate-chassis feature of the old Mk VII family. Sturdy, practical and conventional at the time the Mk VII was designed, by the late 1950s the separate-chassis layout had virtually disappeared, except in North America.

By the late 1950s the technique of producing unit-construction body/chassis structures for saloons (monocoques, in another term) was well-proven, particularly at the Pressed Steel Co. Ltd, who had been making such shells for Morris Motors, Rootes and Standard-Triumph since the late 1930s. Like other smaller companies, however, Jaguar had waited for many years before following the same route, for the tooling costs of an all-new monocoque shell were still very high.

Sir William Lyons, whose eye for a balance sheet was unrivalled, resisted the new trend as long as he could, until Bill Heynes convinced him of the merits of a monocoque structure for the 2.4-litre/3.4-litre models. Even then it must have hurt Jaguar's (for which read 'Sir William's') pocket badly: at a Jaguar function in the late 1950s I remember him facing his workforce and making a morale-raising speech. He assured everyone that he would continue to invest in new models, but that: '... to tool up for a new bodyshell will cost £1 million'.

Lyons knew, however, that by ditching the separate chassis which had featured on the Mk VII family (and, in modified form, on the XK120/XK140/XK150 sports cars), his team would not only be able to save a lot of weight, but could also package a car which was several inches lower than before.

As with the monocoque 2.4-litre/3.4-litre cars which preceded it, therefore, 'Zenith' work began around a wooden mock-up in Fred Gardner's secret body shop. The style was everything and the installation of the running gear would have to follow on after that. Engineering design teams in today's multinational concerns would have been horrified, but this was the way things were habitually done!

Little except the most basic mechanical layout work was tackled until Lyons had established its shape. That layout work, in hardware terms, meant having engine, gearbox and rear suspension units in place and on hand in the workshop, so that they could be rigged up inside the mock-up to ensure clearances.

By taking his time in settling the style of 'Zenith', Sir William cleverly avoided the short period in Britain when other designers were tempted to include rear fins in their styles, and to make their new cars craggy, aping what Detroit was doing in the late 1950s. Mercedes-Benz, for one, fell for fins at this time and may have regretted it. Cleverly, Lyons kept on refining the shapes

he had already developed for the Mk 2 saloons; 'Zenith', though very large, was also smooth and nicely detailed.

In fact students of Jaguar styling of the period – which, in effect, means interpreting what Lyons was thinking – can see that his 'Zenith' style also affected what he was planning for a further derivative of the Mk 2 model – the S-Type. 'Zenith' – the Mk X as I must now begin to call it – clearly influenced the looks of the rear of the S-Type, and when the S-Type evolved further into the 420/Sovereign shape the resemblance between the two different cars was almost uncanny.

The Mk X's shape, though vast, was certainly the smoothest yet seen on a Jaguar saloon. Viewed from the side there was one long, smooth and continuous sweep of wing

By 1959 the 'Zenith' shape was well on its way to finalization. In side view it is right, but there is still some work to be done around the nose, where the now-familiar hooded lamps had not been styled. Sir William Lyons (far right) and Fred Gardner survey their handiwork on a bleak winter's day at Browns Lane.

crown line, linking the headlamps to the tail-lamp clusters. Details such as the window profiles – front, rear and side – were not only reminiscent of the smaller Mk 2 model, but because of the side window layout there were even slight echoes of Mk VII along those flanks.

Although the rear of the car was finalized first, Sir William took time, and looked at several different versions, before settling on a front style. Personally, and having seen various pictures of the mock-up, I prefer ear-lier layouts to the forward leaning version finally chosen. The huge bonnet hinged from the front, so that when it was open it gave easy access to every component in the engine bay. There were hooded headlamps, but I always thought that these were more suited to American cars than to the Mk X. You only have to look at the latest Lincolns and Chryslers of that period to see where that influence came from.

Working on the basis that passengers had to be given as much space as possible, Lyons's

The front end of the Mk X leaned aggressively forward and featured that fashionable early-1960s detail of hooded headlamps. The entire front end / inner headlamps / bonnet panel could be hinged forward to give access to the engine bay.

In the 1950s and 1960s Lucas held a virtual stranglehold over British industry as far as lamp design and supply was concerned. It took ages to bring them to production, these Mk X assemblies being settled and released for tooling even before the body style was finally settled.

Mk X style was radically lower than the Mk IX, but a lot wider; and it carried on the trend begun with the Mk V and followed up with the Mk VII cabin. To put it crudely, having squashed the roof down rather more than the deletion of the chassis frame allowed, he was

obliged to let the flanks grow wider, and even though the doors on this body were almost ludicrously thick, there was certainly a lot more space in the cabin than the Mk VIII/Mk IX had ever offered.

'Mk IV' owners would have been impressed. Here is a simple comparison between the basic critical dimensions of the Mk X and the old Mk IX:

Dimension (in)	Mk X	Mk IX
Styled	1948/9	1959/60
Wheelbase	120 (3,048mm)	120 (3,048mm)
Overall length	202 (5.13m)	196.5 (4.99m)
Overall width	76.3 (1.93m)	73.5 (1.87m)
Overall height	54.5 (1.38m)	62 (1.57m)
Width across front seat	57.5 (1.46m)	53 (1.35m)
Width across rear seat	57.0 (1.45m)	59 (1.50m)
Headroom in driver's seat	38.5 (0.98m)	36 (0.91m)
Headroom in rear seat	33.5 (0.85m)	35 (0.89m)

With the exception of one critical place – there being less headroom in the back seat than before – the Mk X had a rather more spacious cabin and a larger boot. Although the Mk X looked wide – and it was wide, make no mistake – it was only wider overall by 2.8in (7cm). Inside the car, though, there was a much more noticeable increase.

Since it was such a large car which cast such a massive shadow – it was the longest and widest Jaguar ever – many observers missed the startling fact that the Mk X's roof was 7.5in (19cm) lower than that of the Mk IX. That figure, if no other, confirmed the decision to go to a monocoque construction,

Newly minted Mk X bodyshells at the Pressed Steel factory, almost ready to be loaded on to transporters, for delivery to Jaguar in Coventry.

Mk X body assembly at the Pressed Steel factory, showing the way that large pressings were spot-welded together to produce an ultra-stiff monocoque. Note the massive pressed 'chassis legs' which link the suspension cross-member area to the front bulkhead, and the 'dog-leg' aspect of the front screen pillars.

for much of that gain had come from elimi-
nating the separate chassis frame, the rest
by re-packaging the interior.

The new shell was by far the stiffest that
Jaguar or Pressed Steel (who carried out
much of the structural engineering, before
providing body press tools and all supplies
of completed shells) had ever designed.
Much of the strength – beam stiffness and
torsional rigidity – came from the massive
longitudinal sills, whose cross-section was
7 x 7in (18 x 18cm) – allied to a rock-solid
transmission tunnel, sturdy cross-beams
under the front and rear seats and big structural members surrounding the engine bay,
linking those 'chassis legs' to the bulkhead.

Looking back with more than thirty years
of hindsight, it is easy to suggest that this
was an over-engineered shell, but as it was
the very first chassis-less 'Big Jaguar',
Heynes's team could not afford to take
chances. In basic layout there were many
similarities with the shell of the smaller Mk
IIs – and in spite of its size the Mk X would
weigh in at 3,990lb (1,810kg), almost exactly the same figure as the old Mk IX.

TECHNICAL INNOVATION

When the time came to settle the mechanical layout of the new car, the basic specification almost wrote itself, yet many observers
were surprised to see how much of the car's
engineering was being shared with the
charismatic new E-Type, which was to be
unveiled just six months earlier than the Mk
X. If the same observers had realized just
how small Jaguar's design and development
team actually was at the time, they would
have seen why this was necessary.

The three-SU derivative of the famous
3.8-litre XK engine was in exactly the same
tune as that chosen for the new E-Type
sports car, the choice of transmissions –
four-speed manual, optional Laycock over-

drive, or optional Borg Warner automatic
transmission – was the same as on the Mk
IIs and on the old Mk IX, while the independent rear suspension was a further development of the new E-Type system. If only the
pundits had realized it, much of this was
also due to be shared by the Mk II-based S-
Type when it appeared two years later. The
only all-new developments were in the front
suspension area, though the Mk IX-type
Burman power-assisted steering system was
retained.

There was never any suggestion of using
torsion bar front suspension of the type
which Jaguar had favoured on XKs, E-Types
and the Mk VII/VIII/IX family. One reason
was that torsion bars, so expensive to produce, were also much more difficult to 'package' in a unit-construction shell; the other
was that the coil spring and wishbone layout
used on Mk Is and Mk IIs had already
proved to be very satisfactory.

To suppress sound and vibrations as
much as possible (in later years Ford would
invent the acronym NVH – noise, vibration
and harshness), a separate cross-member
was required. Jaguar, like many other of
Europe's car-makers, had been vastly
impressed by the refinement of the new
Peugeot 404, whose cross-beam was a cast-
iron item linking the coil spring/wishbone
units, so the Mk X copied this layout; the
beam was fixed to the bodyshell by two V-
shaped rubber mountings, one under each
monocoque chassis leg. It also helped that
such an I-section beam could be made considerably smaller than a pressed box-section
item like that of the Mk II.

Power steering, of Burman manufacture,
with a Hobourn Eaton engine-driven pump,
was standard, this being of the old Mk IX
type. Surprisingly, it still took four and a
half turns of finger-light action to get the
wheels from lock to lock limits.

It was at the rear of the car, though, that
Jaguar made the biggest advance in this

Kissing cousins? Actually yes, for the E-Type and the Mk X models, both of them launched in 1961, shared the same triple-carburettor 3.8-litre XK engine tune, manual transmission and rear axle assemblies, plus the same basic type of independent rear suspension system. It was economies of scale like this which made it possible for Jaguar to make profits with a relatively limited output.

new saloon car. Not only was this the very first Jaguar saloon to have independent rear suspension (the S-Type would follow two years later), but the entire system was merely an enlarged version of that recently premiered on the sensational E-Type sports car.

The entire independent suspension assembly was carried inside a complex pressed steel 'bridge' structure, which was itself fixed to the body-shell by V-shaped rubber mountings. Inside that bridge was the Salisbury-type rear axle assembly, fixed length driveshafts, tubular forked lower arms and not one, but two combined coil spring/damper units on each side. In its

basic geometry this was a transverse double wishbone system which spread the loads widely, allowing a soft ride with accurate control of the geometry.

The basic layout dated back a long way into Jaguar's history, for similar systems had been proposed by development engineer Bob Knight in the 1940s. The general layout had been conceived in 1955 (following up the De Dion axle tried out on racing D-Types of the period), but the original direct mounting of the axle to the structure always caused too much sound transmission, which led to the inclusion of a rubber-mounted bridge.

Following a lot of testing, it was decided to use independent rear suspension under

Bob Knight

When Bob Knight took over as Jaguar's sole technical chief, his daunting task was to follow the legend of Bill Heynes. It was typical of Knight that this never seemed to trouble him, for he retained the same genial, patient, rather schoolmasterly manner until the day he retired in 1980. By then he had also been Jaguar's Managing Director for the last two years of his career.

The young Knight worked briefly at Standard before joining Jaguar in 1944. By the early 1950s his skills as a design and development engineer were well known, and he became Chief Development Engineer, reporting direct to Bill Heynes during that period.

In those days he operated in what would now be seen as ludicrously modest and ill-equipped premises at Browns Lane, in a building which not only looked after road car testing and development, but which also housed the 'works' motorsport department.

By that time he had already figured strongly in chassis design for the C-Type and D-Type racing sports cars, and in the next few years it was his fanatical attention to testing detail, not least in regard to ride quality and refinement, which made all the Big Jaguar saloons so phenomenally quiet and capable.

My abiding memory of Bob Knight is of a polite and civilized man, often to be seen with a half-smile on his face, who enjoyed the explanation and exposition of his job – a man who would have been truly at home as a professor in a lecture theatre.

He seemed to have infinite patience and would far rather see a new model launch delayed than have to release something which, in his eyes, was not yet ready for sale.

Bob Knight, Jaguar's chief development engineer for many years, takes much credit for the remarkable refinement and ride boasted by the Mk X. Even though this was such a large car, there is no doubt that the Mk X was an extremely capable road car.

neither as cheap, nor as simple, as vast companies like Ford or General Motors could have made it – but, then, such firms would probably never even have attempted independent suspension at all!

Those 14in road wheels, incidentally, which had been chosen for the new car well before the styling was settled, were the smallest ever used on a Jaguar up to that time, and they would prove to be the smallest of all time, for the XJ6 models which took over in 1968 used 15in wheels once again.

Although the 3.8-litre engine destined for the Mk X was a lot more powerful than that used in the Mk IX, there would be no

the new E-Type sports car. Then a very brave strategic move was the decision to incorporate developments of this layout under all the new Jaguar saloon car ranges being planned for the 1960s. Perhaps it was

Long, low, very wide, but somehow slightly ponderous – this was the Mk X model, as introduced in 1961.

changes to the line-up of transmission options for the first few years (although in the very early stages it was thought that manual transmission should not be offered). Most production cars were ordered with the Borg Warner automatic transmission, and it would be some years before Jaguar even loaned out an 'overdrive' Mk X to the press so that performance figures could be taken.

The torquey 3.8-litre engine, in any case, was a great low-speed slogger and thus ideally suited to automatic transmission, but its growing reluctance to rev freely was

becoming more obvious, now that more modern designs were beginning to appear under rivals' bonnets.

Like the Mk IX (and the current smaller Mk IIs), the new car was also equipped with four-wheel Dunlop disc brakes, along with a unique type of servo. This design, from Kelsey-Hayes of North America, was made under licence in the UK by Dunlop. Whereas engine vacuum provided the motive power for the boost in the usual way, there was a mechanical bell crank from the servo to the pedal itself. According to Jaguar, this meant that if the servo should fail (it did, persistently, and there was a spongy feel at low speeds too) the braking system would merely revert to manual, unassisted, mode.

PUBLIC LAUNCH

When the Mk X was finally introduced, it got something of a mixed reception. There was no doubt that its style came as a shock to some observers, particular as it followed the appearance of the long, low and lean E-Type, and the neat and compact transformation of the Mk1into the Mk 2 saloon range.

The fact is that the Mk X was the widest British car on the market, one of the heaviest, and had rather massive, bulbous looks which would take some time to be accepted. Unlike other new European cars of the day, too, it was not at all flamboyant (no fins, no big creases, no flashy colour schemes) – just very, very large.

Even when the Mk X was introduced, in October 1961, it was still not quite ready to go on sale, for Jaguar had not really given Pressed Steel enough time to complete, prove and 'shake-down' the bodyshell tooling. This meant that there was ample time for the design to be analysed before deliveries got under way at the end of the year.

Having left Jaguar before the Mk X was introduced, but after prototype testing had begun, I was privileged to watch its reception with a degree of inside knowledge. It

---

Jaguar Mk X 3.8-litre (1961–4)

Numbers built
13,382

Layout
Unit-construction steel body/chassis structure. Five-seater, front engine/rear drive, sold as four-door saloon or limousine

Engine

Type	Jaguar XK
Block material	Cast iron
Head material	Cast aluminium
Cylinders	6 in-line
Cooling	Water
Bore and stroke	87 x 106mm
Capacity	3,781cc
Main bearings	7
Valves	2 per cylinder, operated by twin ohcand inverted bucket-type tappets
Compression ratio	9.0:1 (or optional 8.0:1)
Carburettors	3 SU 2in
Max. power	265bhp @ 5,500rpm
Max. torque	260lb/ft @ 4,000rpm

Transmission
Four-speed manual gearbox, with synchromesh on top, third and second gears

Clutch	Single dry plate; hydraulically operated

Internal gearbox ratios

Top	1.00
3rd	1.365
2nd	1.98
1st	3.37
Reverse	3.37
Final drive	3.54:1

Overdrive (Laycock) was optional, on top gear only, when the final drive ratio became 3.77:1. Internal transmission ratio was:

Top (O/D)	0.778

Automatic transmission (Borg Warner) was optional. Internal gearbox ratios were :

Direct	1.00
Intermediate	1.44
Low	2.31
Reverse	2.0
Maximum torque multiplication	2.15
Final drive ratio	3.54:1

Suspension and steering

Front	Independent, coil springs, wishbones, anti-roll bar, telescopic dampers
Rear	Independent, double coil springs, fixed length drive shafts, lower wishbones, radius arms, double telescopic dampers
Steering	Recirculating ball, power-assisted
Tyres	7.50–14in cross-ply
Wheels	Steel disc, bolt-on
Rim width	5.5in

Brakes

Type	Disc brakes at front and rear, with vacuum servo assistance
Size	10.75in diameter front, 10in diameter rear

Dimensions (in/mm)

Track	
Front	58/1,473
Rear	58/1,473
Wheelbase	120/3,048
Overall length	202/5,130
Overall width	76.3/1,938
Overall height	54.5/1,384
Unladen weight	3,990lb/1,820kg

was interesting to see that many pundits' opinions were shared with those of Jaguar staff – though staff-men rarely felt bold enough to voice them to Bill Heynes and Sir William Lyons!

Although the newspapers and magazines did their best to welcome the new car (*Autocar* headlined its description: 'Finest Jaguar Yet'), most of them preferred to test this vast machine before finally making up their minds. By using what was, in effect, a split-bench front seat, and very soft suspension, it could be argued that the Mk X had gone too 'transatlantic'. Were the designers right to go back to using an American-style 'T-handle' for the hand (parking) brake? Was this car, they collectively wondered, too large and too heavy for the market place?

Compared with the old Mk IX the new Mk X was 5.7in (14.5cm) longer, 3.3in (8.5cm) wider, and no less than 8.5in (21.5cm) lower – though it was almost exactly the same weight as before. With so much more power (265bhp gross instead of 220bhp, along with an extra 40lb/ft of torque), and what was assumed to be a better aerodynamic shape, it promised to be a lot faster – but would it hold the road?

There was also time for the media to wonder why there appeared to be little mechanical innovation – no new engines and no new transmissions for instance – which rather led many to ignore the car's excellent standard of equipment. In addition, by comparison with the last of the Mk IXs, which sold for £1,939 in the UK, the price had shot up to no less than £2,393, and that was even before 'essential' extras like overdrive and/or automatic transmission were specified.

MK X ON SALE

Although a crop of teething troubles had to be sorted out first, Mk X deliveries finally

began in the winter of 1961/2, which must have been a great relief to everyone at the factory, as E-Type production was still at a low ebb, and the business was certainly not operating to capacity. Jaguar's own records confirm this lull in deliveries: 1960/1, 24,018; 1961/2, 22,030.

To the relief of all Jaguar enthusiasts and long-time owners, the Mk X proved to be a large car which also handled very well indeed. Owing to the chassis being completely power-assisted, the brakes required little effort and the steering was almost too light and it took little effort to urge the 4,000lb (1,800kg) car along.

There was no doubt, however, that the choice of chassis settings – Jaguar hoped that they would appeal to American customers without offending British and European tastes – was always going to be controversial. The ride was very soft indeed, and in spite of the way most British testers tended to give Jaguar the benefit of any doubt they still felt obliged to comment that 'At times one could wish for stronger damping to counteract slow-rate, longitudinal "plunge", as distinct from "pitch" …'.

Of the steering, too, there were mixed opinions, for the best that *The Autocar* testers could think of to say was that:

> reactions among the test staff to the power-assisted steering were mixed, but the synopsis of opinion was broadly as follows. Most important, it improves with acquaintance … it was voted too low-geared about the straight-ahead position, and at low speeds lacks the sensitivity that makes for relaxation. The faster it goes, the better it is ….

The first time I drove a Mk X – an automatic transmission version, in 1962, I was daunted by its sheer size, for it seemed an awfully long way from the driving seat to the left front corner. In addition, I couldn't gauge the length behind the rear window

Even though the Mk X/420G was such a large car, there was no more than average rear seat leg room – although that seat was exceptionally wide.

The Mk X had an extremely wide cabin, the front seat area straddling a substantial central transmission tunnel. In 1961 this was the most co-ordinated Jaguar instrument panel so far offered, but there was still no sign of padding or other safety provisions. The vast majority of all Mk Xs, by the way, had automatic transmission, like this particular example. The position of the steering wheel was adjustable for reach.

glass – all in all I was rather terrified by its bulk.

American drivers, on the other hand, were not, for by current Cadillac, Lincoln or Oldsmobile standards (the obvious competition) this was actually a smaller car. Even the mass-market USA, Fords and Chevrolets were as big, though by no means as fast or as well equipped.

But it wasn't merely the car's overall size which was daunting – there was also the great apparent size of the interior. The Mk X was much wider across front and rear seats, so much so that carrying three-abreast in the back seat was quite straightforward. When I once picked up a young National Serviceman to give him a lift back from London to Coventry, he relaxed on the other side of the split-bench front seat, so far away that I was almost tempted to raise my voice when I chatted to him.

Those large front seats, by the way, were distinctly a mixed blessing. Large enough for the fattest tycoon to lounge in great comfort, they were not at all supportive. From the day the car was delivered the leather coverings were very slippery, and unless safety belts were fitted (very few cars had them in the early 1960s) it was all too easy for the driver to slip from side to side as the car changed direction.

Independent road tests soon showed up

the big performance gains from Mk IX to Mk X. The new car had a top speed of 120mph (193km/h) and although it was possible to force the fuel economy down to 13 or 14mpg (20 or 22l/100km), that didn't seem to matter in those days, when petrol cost only about 4/- (20p) an Imperial gallon.

Surprisingly, those low sleek looks cannot have been very aerodynamically efficient – though since the drag coefficient does not seem to have been measured, we may never know how awful it was – for the lofty Mk IX's top speed was 114mph (184km/h), with a nominal 45bhp less to urge it along.

This detail of the rear compartment of the Mk X shows the twin fold-down picnic tables, the twin ashtrays, and the air vents feeding heated air through from the heating system.

Here, in summary, is how independent tests of the two types compared:

Performance	Mk X	Mk IX
Top speed (mph)	119.5	114.2
	(192km/h)	(184km/h)
Acceleration (secs):		
0–30	4.9	4.2
0–60	9.1	11.3
0–80	20.6	18.6
0–100	33.3	34.8
Standing start ¼-mile (secs)		
	18.5	18.1
Overall fuel consumption		
(Imperial mpg)	14.1	13.5
	(20l/100km)	(21l/100km)

In fact the Mk X soon settled down, selling as well in 'Empire' territories overseas as in the USA, and a whole series of development changes were made to the specification in the next three years.

Most buyers loved the Mk X for its spaciousness, for the 'Olde Worlde' atmosphere of the interior, complete with expanses of polished walnut and Connolly leather. The picnic tables built into the back of the front seats were a nice touch, but it can be questioned whether they were regularly used.

By 1964 there was no doubt that the Mk X was a better car than it had been two years earlier, though the company never had any need to trumpet that fact. Jaguar's problem, in fact, was that motoring standards were being raised all the time, and the running gear which had been thought so advanced in the 1950s was now beginning to show its age.

MK X (4.2-LITRE)

Many Jaguar enthusiasts insist that the revised Mk X which appeared in October 1961 was the car which Jaguar should have

offered in the first place. It is a nice thought, but it means little, for the hardware which made all the difference – the 4.2-litre engine and the all-new gearbox – had not been designed in 1961, so such action would not have been possible!

In fact Jaguar made several across-the-range changes in the autumn of 1964, long planned, which meant that not only the Mk X, but also the E-Type and the Mk II/S-Types all benefited. Not only the larger version of the famous XK engine, but the new all-synchromesh gearbox and a different type of Borg Warner automatic transmission were all made available at the same time.

For the Mk X it was major-redesign time, for in addition there was a new and more advanced steering system, better brakes and shortly afterwards the launch of a limousine version too.

By the early 1960s the XK engine had been in existence for nearly twenty years and had become something of an icon around Jaguar. One day, for sure, it would have to be replaced, but for the time being Sir William Lyons wanted to continue squeezing every penny out of his investment. The sales force was still happy to market any car with one or other version installed, while the design team thought there was more to come from the long-established layout.

By this time there appeared to be a ready-made alternative to the XK engine within the group, for Jaguar had absorbed Daimler in 1960, to find that they had inherited not one, but two brand-new Daimler 90-degree engine designs. One of them, a 2½-litre unit, was used in the Daimler SP250, while a larger 4½-litre power plant found a home in the Daimler Majestic Major and Limousine models.

Although Jaguar dabbled with the idea of using the 4½-litre V8 in the Mk X, this scheme never got far. For one reason, by XK standards it was backward-looking, with

163

By the time the largest Jaguar had become the 420G, XK engines had inherited ribbed camshaft covers. The impressive triple 2in SU carburettor installation was standard on all these cars, and that is the radiator header tank closest to the camera.

ohv valve gear, with more torque but nominally less top-end power, but there was also the uncomfortable fact that it was not tooled up for serious mass production.

One Mk X development car was fitted with the big Daimler unit with rather startling results (the car's performance improved considerably, which tells us a lot about the relative power claims of each company!), but the project was never taken seriously.

Although Walter Hassan had rejoined Jaguar (from Coventry-Climax), along with Harry Mundy, his long-time partner at that resourceful little firm, neither had much influence on the development of the 4.2-litre

XK engine, which was almost ready for production when they arrived.

The bald figures suggested that only a simple bore increase had been needed to enlarge the XK engine from 3,781cc to 4,235cc, but the truth was more complex. To find space for the extra 0.2in (5.07mm) bore, the engine's entire internal layout had been rejigged. A new block casting was needed, for the cylinder centres had moved around, the bores joined together and the cooling flows improved. Naturally this meant that a different crankshaft was needed, though somehow the 3.8-type cylinder head casting and stud locations were retained.

Jaguar Mk X 4.2-litre (1964–6)

Jaguar 420G (1966–70)

Numbers built
5,137 Mk X 4.2-litre (this includes 18 limousines)
5,763 420G (this includes 24 limousines)

Layout
Unit-construction steel body/chassis structure. Five-seater, front engine/rear drive, sold as four-door saloon or limousine

Engine
Type	Jaguar XK
Block material	Cast iron
Head material	Cast aluminium
Cylinders	6 in-line
Cooling	Water
Bore and stroke	92.07 x 106mm
Capacity	4,235cc
Main bearings	7
Valves	2 per cylinder, operated by twin ohc, and inverted bucket-type tappets
Compression ratio	8.0:1 (or optional 9.0:1 or 7.0:1)
Carburettors	3 SU 2in
Max. power	265bhp @ 5,400rpm
Max. torque	275lb/ft @ 4,000rpm

Transmission
Four-speed manual gearbox, with synchromesh on all forward gears

Clutch	Diaphragm spring; hydraulically operated

Internal gearbox ratios
Top	1.00
3rd	1.328
2nd	1.973
1st	3.04
Reverse	3.49
Final drive	3.54:1

Overdrive (Laycock) was optional, on top gear only, when the final drive ratio became 3.77:1. Internal transmission ratio was :

Top (O/D)	0.778

165

Automatic transmission (Borg Warner) was optional. Internal gearbox ratios were :

Direct	1.00
Intermediate	1.44
Low	2.31
Reverse	2.0
Maximum torque multiplication	2.15
Final drive ratio	3.54:1

Suspension and steering

Front	Independent, coil springs, wishbones, anti-roll bar, telescopic dampers
Rear	Independent, double coil springs, fixed length drive shafts, lower wishbones, radius arms, double telescopic dampers
Steering	Worm and follower, power-assisted
Tyres	205–14in radial-ply
Wheels	Steel disc, bolt-on
Rim width	5.5in

Brakes

Type	Disc brakes at front and rear, with vacuum servo assistance
Size	10.9in diameter front, 10.38in diameter rear

Dimensions (in/mm)

Track	
Front	58/1,473
Rear	58/1,473
Wheelbase	120/3,048
Overall length	202/5,130
Overall width	76.3/1,938
Overall height	54.5/1,384
Unladen weight	3,990lb/1,820kg

Jaguar also retained the same triple-SU carburettor fuelling arrangements and claimed that there was a torque improvement throughout the speed range, with no loss of high-revving capability, though today's Jaguar drivers will probably tell you a different story. Certainly the 4.2-litre engine did not rev as freely as its smaller-capacity forebears, particularly in later years when the first power-sapping changes had to be made to satisfy early exhaust emission regulations.

Along with the use of an electrical alter-nator, a separately-mounted power-steering pump, a Lucas pre-engaged starter, a Holset viscous coupling for the cooling fan drive, and a diaphragm spring clutch, this was a thoroughly redesigned and updated engine.

The other innovation was the launch of another major new mechanical 'building block', a new four-speed all-synchromesh gearbox. By any standards it was a great advance on the ancient Moss-type gearbox which Jaguar had been machining since the 1940s. Even when it was modern, the Moss-type box had been criticized for having a

The Mk X's spare wheel just– and only just – fitted inside the shallow boot compartment. This car also had twin tanks, each one tucked into the recess of the rear wing: there were two linked filler caps, mounted immediately behind the rear window.

slow, easily beaten synchromesh; by the 1960s this, and the lack of first-gear synchro, was unsupportable.

Although little mention had been made of it at the time, Jaguar had built an all-synchromesh gearbox for the D-Type race cars as early as 1954, so there was a great deal of experience with this layout before a new road-car came along in 1964. The unit was robust and neatly detailed, and would eventually be used in all manual-transmission Jaguars built until the late 1970s.

However, because a large and increasing percentage of Mk X customers wanted automatic transmission in their cars, few of them ever tried the new manual gearbox, with or without overdrive. Instead they chose Borg Warner automatic, probably not realizing that it was a new design – Model 8 instead of Model DG – and not caring that there was still some slippage and fuel economy loss when the torque converter was doing its job.

Owing to all the publicity surrounding these new fittings, the use of a new Marles Varamatic Bendix power-assisted steering system, and the use of a conventional vacuum servo for the braking system, almost went by unnoticed. Not only did the power-steering have more direct steering towards the extreme of lock than around the straight ahead, but it also meant that a lot less steering wheel twirling was required in day-to-day use. Instead of the original car's four and a quarter turns, the Marles system required only two and three-quarter turns from lock to lock.

There were no changes to the Mk X's style at this time, and after a very brief overlap on the assembly lines the 4.2-litre car took over completely in October 1964. In fact Jaguar must have been slightly anxious about the new car's impact, for most surprisingly it made an automatic transmission car immediately available to *Autocar* for road test.

Performance	Mk X (3.8-litre)	Mk X (4.2-litre)
Top speed (mph)	119.5 (192km/h)	121.5 (196km/h)
Acceleration (secs)		
0–30mph	4.9	4.0
0–60mph	9.1	9.9
0–80mph	20.6	17.0
0–100mph	33.3	27.4
Standing start ¼-mile (secs)	18.5	17.0
Overall fuel consumption (Imperial mpg)	14.1	14.5

Jaguar's marketing stance had always been that the 4.2-litre engine was not meant to provide more power, but more torque, so there was no disappointment with a 121.5mph (196km/h) top speed. For Jaguar, though, the good news was that this large and heavy car accelerated more speedily than before, yet used less fuel.

It was predictable, therefore, that the testers should rave over the latest car, pointing out that:

Spaciousness, comfort and a very high performance remain the chief selling points of the Jaguar Mk X, and in the new 4.2-litre these are now allied to more precise control to go with the extra power. The price is in the usual Jaguar tradition of exceptional value for money.

It was a test full of praise (almost, one feels, of relief after the less-than-superb impression left by the earlier Mk X), the car being described as covering the ground 'in the forceful, tireless manner of the smaller Mk 2 models ... Engine smoothness and quietness are as good as ever …'. The steering was described as 'a revelation' and even the heating system (always known to be a blind spot on 1950s-design Jaguars) was thought to be 'far better'.

The major update, in other words, had been well worthwhile, for it allowed the Mk X to continue, serenely, as Jaguar's flagship for a time, especially as full air-conditioning became a £275 option from mid-1965. The flagship image was further enhanced in October 1965 when a limousine version of the car was unveiled. This was very much a hand-built (one almost wrote 'coachbuilt') version of the standard machine, with a new design of front seat where extra rear-seat leg-room was claimed – what this meant was that the poor chauffeur was going to be allowed a little less space than the owner-driver expected!

A sound-proof division was incorporated in the back of the front seats, this having sliding safety glass panels, twin flush-fitting writing tables and a radio console. Although the price increase was small – the Limousine sold for £193 more than the saloon – very few

Although the Mk X/420G style came first, Sir William Lyons was still happy enough to use a development of a very successful theme on the smaller and more compact Jaguar 420/Daimler Sovereign model introduced in 1966. Having started life as the Mk II range of 1959, this was the final development of a very successful theme, and its 'through-wingline' styling similarities to the Mk X were obvious.

were ever constructed. Jaguar's records show that there were just eighteen built on the 4.2-litre Mk X base, and a further twenty-four on the final 420G base.

420G

By the time the Mk X gave way to the 420G – the same car really with minor improvements – Jaguar had already decided that there would be no more Big Jaguars. The design of the new XJ6 model had already been settled, a car which was meant to take

over from every existing Jaguar saloon, and there were no plans to diversify again.

Fresh from its merger with BMC, Jaguar chose October 1966 to add yet more complication to its model range. While continuing every existing range of models, the company introduced yet another variation on the Mk II/S-Type theme called the 420, and displaced the Mk X by the 420G. The last Mk X, by the way, was built two months after the 420G appeared.

As far as the biggest Jaguar was concerned, however, there was little to get excited about. The 420G was effectively the

Sir William Lyons always took a lot of time to settle the decorative detail of his cars. Note, here, that the 420G number plate is neatly encased by a Jaguar badge, reverse lamps, a boot lid lock and badging.

The 420G was the first Big Jaguar to feature any sort of padding around its instruments. The location of the clock is particularly neat, as is the labelling of the line of control switches.

From 1966 to 1970 the Mk X was renamed 420G, the only external visual change being the addition of a slim chromium strip along the flanks. The '420G' nomenclature was never placarded on the car.

old Mk X with a very minor makeover, for there were no important style changes and the running gear was precisely as before.

What the 'G' meant Jaguar certainly never explained, though the '420' undoubtedly referred to the 4.2-litre engine. In view of the car's size, 'G' probably stood for 'Grand' (or, as Mercedes-Benz had often stated for their largest models, 'Grosse'), but the customers were left to guess. That one letter, at least, served to distinguish the final 'Zenith' development from the smaller Jaguar 420, whose ancestry was totally different, but which looked remarkably similar from some angles.

There were a few ways – not many – to 'pick' the 420G from the last of the Mk Xs. For the 420G, Jaguar added a slim chrome strip along the crease in the body side panels and specified a slightly different front grille which incorporated a thick central chrome stripe (rather like that of the smaller 420 model).

Inside the car, where the cabin was virtually unchanged, there were padded crash rolls on the door panels below the windows and atop the facia, which also supported a clock above the centre console. But that was

really all – the very rare limousine option was carried on and even the British price remained unchanged at £2,238.

Thus retouched, the 420G carried on serenely for another four years and was quite unaffected by the formation of British Leyland, when Jaguar began to slide towards anonymity. By the summer of 1970, though, it had certainly become forgotten by all but Jaguar's dealer staff themselves. XJ6 fever had set in, impatient queues had built up in many countries and the sheer elegance and capability of the new car overshadowed older types.

Like its predecessor, the Mk X, the 420G sold steadily (rather than well) but consistently, though I question whether it was ever profitable for the company to persevere with it. At their height in the early 1960s, about 110 Mk Xs were being sold every week, but that figure fell steadily during the decade. In four years a total of 5,763 420Gs were built, which means that in an average week only about thirty such cars were built. The end came in June 1970, when any space left by departing 420Gs was instantly taken up by more and yet more XJ6s. So, what was all the fuss about?

9 After the 420G: XJ6 Takes Over

By the early 1960s Jaguar was building far too many different models and a decision to rationalize was overdue. This was surely not a pre-planned situation, rather one which had developed with time. Even though nearly every car was powered by one or other derivative of the famous XK engine, the planners had to find ways to mix and match several bodies, badges and engine sizes with many options, colours and destinations.

In 1964/5, for instance, the company sold 24,601 cars, but no fewer than twelve Jaguars and closely-related Daimlers were listed. At any one time in the late 1960s, the Browns Lane factory saw E-Types, Mk 2/S/420/Sovereign and 420G models all being built in the same limited space. If there was a strategy, it was not obvious. Even though many of these cars were based on one basic versatile design, the Mk 2/S-Type, it made no economic sense for this to continue.

By 1964, in fact, we now know that Sir William Lyons was ready to sweep away all this complexity. It was at this point that he made a very brave decision – not only to replace, say, the Mk X/420G or the Mk 2/S-Type/420 range, but to replace both of them at the same time with a new unit-construction saloon. The result was the XJ6, which became by far the most successful car ever produced by Jaguar. Even so, this change did not actually happen cleanly – not instantly, not surgically, and not without temporarily adding even more complexity to the assembly lines at Browns Lane in 1968.

It took so long for the new 'XJ4' (as it was originally known) to be finalized, that Jaguar was obliged to buy time by upgrading the S-Type into the 420 model, and the Mk X into the 420G. In the event it is true that the old Mk 2 and S disappeared before the XJ6 was launched in 1968, but in the event the 420 continued in 'Daimler Sovereign' guise for another year, while the 420G remained in production for a further two years.

Even so, from the late 1960s Sir William's intention was to see Jaguar building only one basic saloon, and one sports car. His design team, in fact, was so small that only one new project could have been tackled at this time. Effectively, this meant that the engineers would be obliged to evolve an extremely versatile new model – one which could not only replace the very large Mk X/420G in due course, but one which would also replace the old 2.4-litre Mk 2 as well. It was a tall order.

AFTER THE MK X

The inevitable result, a new car originally coded XJ4, but eventually launched in 1968 as the XJ6/Daimler Sovereign series, was a new model smaller than the Mk X/420G, but larger than the Mk II/S range, which meant that there was really to be no direct replacement for the Mk X/420G model.

In many ways it was always likely that the new XJ6 would lean a little more

172

Jaguar Sales: 1945 to 1970

Here are Jaguar's production achievements, by Jaguar financial year, for the years covering the 'Big Jaguars' described in this book. Note that 'Jaguar-Daimler'-badged cars are also included in these totals:

Year ending	Home market	Export market	Total
1946 (31 July)	816	316	1,132
1947	3,393	949	4,342
1948	2,013	2,173	4,186
1949	2,089	1,224	3,313
1950	2,721	3,926	6,647
1951	1,532	4,273	5,805
1952	1,001	7,978	8,979
1953	2,471	7,643	10,114
1954	4,796	5,335	10,131
1955	4,462	5,438	9,900
1956	5,305	6,847	12,152
1957	6,338	6,614	12,952
1958	8,375	9,177	17,552
1959	10,400	10,476	20,876
1960	9,664	9,677	19,341
1961	13,844	10,174	24,018
1962	10,895	11,135	22,030
1963	12,754	12,235	24,989
1964	14,142	10,206	24,348
1965	15,041	9,560	24,601
1966	13,838	12,098	25,936
1967	10,624	12,026	22,650
1968	14,515	9,800	24,315
1969 (30 Sept – 14 months trading)	12,239	14,970	27,209
1970 (30 Sept)	12,001	18,422	30,423

Note The Mk V was introduced in the 1949 year
The Mk VII was introduced in the 1951 year
The Mk X was introduced in the 1962 year
1961 was the year of the takeover of Daimler
1967 was the year including the merger with BMC
1968 was the year including the foundation of British Leyland
1969 was the year in which new-generation XJ6 assembly began

The XJ6 of 1968 was smaller and lighter, but no less capable than the 420G, which would be rendered obsolete after only two years. The styling was a further, more delicate and extremely attractive version of that introduced on the Mk X.

towards the existing smaller cars than towards the Mk X/420G. 'Big Jaguar' sales were already well over their peak and declining steadily, while Jaguar's profits were buoyed up by the demand for the smaller machines.

In the beginning, it seems, Sir William Lyons planned to use not one, but three, different engines in the new model: a development of the six-cylinder XK unit, along with V8 and V12 derivatives of a brand new engine which Walter Hassan and Harry Mundy (newly returned from several years as *Autocar's* Technical Editor) were in the process of designing.

The rest of the drive line was already

familiar to Jaguar enthusiasts – the all-synchromesh gearbox, the chassis-mounted final drive and the unique cage-mounted independent rear suspension from the Mk X/420G were all modern and would be used again. As ever, Laycock overdrive would be optional, as would Borg Warner automatic transmission.

SHAPING THE NEW CAR

Faced with the need to develop the XJ6 on these lines, you or I could probably have written a specification for it and find that this was very similar to that actually chosen

The mid-1980s Jaguar/Daimler range, even though restyled, retouched and made rather smaller, still had obvious styling links with the Mk X, the last of the 'Big Jaguars'.

by Heynes's team. But making lists was one thing: producing a practical, value-for-money car was quite another.

Jaguar, quite brutally, could not afford to get it wrong, for this project represented their future, particularly in North America where so many sales would have to be won. The demands were such as to make a modern, computer-led multinational design team blanch, but in the 1960s it was a colossal undertaking for what was still quite a small company.

We now know that it took a long time – getting on for two years – for Sir William Lyons and Fred Gardner to settle on the style and the package that they wanted. As ever, the new car took shape as a wooden mock-up, built in a cramped workshop close to (but separated from) the experimental department, and many car park inspections – always carried out at the weekend – were made before Jaguar's founder was satisfied.

Along with Bill Heynes, Lyons's first task was not to shape the car, but to agree the

Jaguar XJ6 assembly at Browns Lane in the 1980s, showing that the basic monocoque structure of the latest car was still broadly the same as that of the Mk X.

Dimension (in)	420G (was Mk X)	XJ6	420 (was S-Type)
Wheelbase	120 (3,048mm)	108.8 (2,764mm)	107.4 (2,728mm)
Overall length	202 (5.13m)	189.5 (4.81m)	187.8 (4.77m)
Overall width	76.3 (1.93m)	69.7 (1.77m)	66.7 (1.69m)
Overall height	54.5 (1.38m)	53.0 (1.35m)	54.5 (1.38m)
Width across front seat	57.5 (1.46m)	54.0 (1.37m)	56.0 (1.42m)
Width across rear seat	57.0 (1.45m)	53.5 (1.36m)	56.0 (1.42m)
Headroom in driver's seat	38.5 (0.98m)	35.5 (0.90m)	37.0 (0.94m)
Headroom in rear seat	33.5 (0.85m)	33.0 (0.84m)	34.0 (0.86m)
Unladen weight (lb)	3,990 (1,810kg)	3,703 (1,680kg)	3,675 (1,667kg)

By the end of the 1980s, the XJ6 family style which had taken over from the Mk X/420G in 1970 was almost ready to be phased out.

By the 1980s the XJ6/XJ12 family had progressed to Series III, this being the Daimler Double Six (V12-engined) version produced in 1986.

platform on which it would be built. Almost by definition, it would have to be larger than the 420 and smaller than the 420G. The table on page 177 shows what was achieved.

What this tells us is that apart from reducing the thickness of its doors (the Mk X/420G doors were admittedly very bulbous), the new XJ6 had not been given a more space-efficient cabin. Front-seat passengers had 3.5in (9cm) less shoulder width to relax in, while the rear-seat space was significantly reduced. Perhaps it was no coincidence that Jaguar would eventually be obliged to produce a longer-wheelbase XJ6, where all the extra space was provided in the back seats.

The original XJ6's wheelbase was, however, 11.2in (284mm) shorter, it was 12.5in (317mm) shorter overall, and there had been a weight saving of nearly 300lb (136kg).

But it wasn't the new car's size, nor entirely its shape, which made it such a great car, but its quite incredible refinement, soothing character and sheer capability. Not only was the XJ6 faster than the 420G had ever been, but it held the road better, handled better, was quieter than ever, and still offered great value for money. Any doubts that the XJ6 could take over from a larger car were swept away as soon as the new models became available.

Appendix A
Daimler Limousine

The next time you see a modern Daimler Limousine in action, try to imagine what is under the skin of that vast and distinctive machine. Hidden away, out of sight, are the much modified floorpan, the suspension units and the running gear of the old Jaguar Mark X/420G models.

Visually, of course, the two cars could not be more different. The 420G was low, wide, bulbous, with sweeping lines, and was definitely a Jaguar. The Daimler Limousine was higher, no less wide, but with totally different styling, particularly at the rear where traces of Hooper-type razor-edge shapes remained; it could only be a Daimler.

There was even more to the Jaguar connection than the chassis. With styling influenced by Sir William Lyons, it was originally assembled by Vanden Plas in north-west London, but from the end of the 1970s final assembly was always located at Jaguar's Browns Lane factory. It was never assembled in the 'Daimler' factory at Radford.

Before delving too far into the complex heritage of the Daimler DS420 Limousine, it is as well to recall that Jaguar bought Daimler in 1960, and joined forces with the British Motor Corporation in 1966. It should also be pointed out that the distinguished London coachbuilders, Vanden Plas, had been absorbed by Austin in 1946 and that Austin was a founding member of BMC.

In the 1950s and 1960s there were three principal British suppliers of limousines to the main users, namely government bodies and officials, tycoons, local authority dignitaries and hire car concerns. Rolls-Royce looked after the expensive end of the market, Daimler took the middle ground, while BMC-based Vanden Plas Princess models swept up the balance of the business.

Rolls-Royce, naturally, does not enter into the complicated commercial manoeuvrings which took place in the mid-1960s, but Daimler and Vanden Plas increasingly came into conflict. The best way to analyse what happened, what had to happen, no less, is to recall the situation in 1966.

Daimler had been in the limousine business for many years and even after the Jaguar takeover development of new models continued. The DR450 model, complete with Daimler's modern 4½-litre V8 engine, was introduced in 1961, and was selling steadily at about 100 cars a year.

Virtually hand-built around a separate chassis with a beam axle and leaf-spring suspension, a long-wheelbase version of the Majestic Major design, the DR450 was a 220bhp machine running on a 138in (3,505mm) wheelbase and weighing about 4,700lb (2,100kg). Styling, which was really a developed version of the Daimler Regency II of 1955, was rounded and graceful. It was assembled at Daimler's Radford factory. If the truth was told, it could never have been a profitable machine at any stage of its life.

BMC's Princess limousine was descended from the old Austin A135, which had been introduced in 1952, and in turn was a descendant of the Sheerline design of 1946. Rebadged in 1957 as a Vanden Plas 4-litre, it had a 120bhp 4-litre overhead-valve Austin engine (shared with several BMC

Daimler Limousine (1968–92)

Numbers built
4,206

Layout

Unit-construction steel body/chassis structure based on lengthened/strengthened Mk X/420G platform. Seven-seater, front engine/rear drive, sold as four-door limousine, or landaulette

Engine
Type	Jaguar XK
Block material	Cast iron
Head material	Cast aluminium
Cylinders	6 in-line
Cooling	Water
Bore and stroke	92.07 x 106mm
Capacity	4,235cc
Main bearings	7
Valves	2 per cylinder, operated by twin ohc,and inverted bucket-type tappets
Compression ratio	8.0:1
Carburettors	2 SU 2in
Max. power	245bhp @ 5,500rpm
Max. torque	282lb/ft @ 3,750rpm

Transmission
Manual transmission not available.

Three-speed Borg Warner automatic transmission

Clutch	Diaphragm spring; hydraulically operated

Internal gearbox ratios
Direct	1.00
Intermediate	1.46
Low	2.40
Reverse	2.0
Maximum torque multiplication	2.0
Final drive ratio	3.54:1

Suspension and steering
Front	Independent, coil springs, wishbones, anti-roll bar, telescopic dampers
Rear	Independent, double coil springs, fixed length drive shafts lower wishbones, radius arms, double telescopic dampers
Steering	Worm and roller, power-assisted
Tyres	H70–HR15in, radial-ply
Wheels	Steel disc, bolt-on
Rim width	6in

Brakes

Type	Disc brakes at front and rear, with vacuum servo assistance
Size	10.9in diameter front, 10.38in diameter rear

Dimensions (in/mm)

Track	
Front	58/1,473
Rear	58/1,473
Wheelbase	141/3,580
Overall length	226/5,740
Overall width	78.5/1,990
Overall height	63.8/1,620
Unladen weight	4,706lb/2,135kg

commercial vehicles and the Jensen 541 range!), ran on a 132in (3,353mm) wheelbase, and weighed about 4,800lb (2,200kg). The styling was pure Vanden Plas, with part razor-edge cabin lines. Although the chassis was an Austin design, final assembly was at Vanden Plas in Kingsbury, North London; this was another car which sold at a mere 100 or150 cars a year.

Immediately after the merger of Jaguar-Daimler and BMC, it was easy to see that these two cars, though with different pedigrees and power outputs, were really in direct competition for a tiny market. At that time the Vanden Plas cost £3,136, while the Daimler sold for £3,553.

Although Vanden Plas had started developing a revised Princess limousine by this time and Sir William Lyons was also toying with the idea of producing a replacement for the Daimler DR450 Limousine, after the Jaguar-BMC merger of 1966 there was no commercial logic in putting both these new cars on the market.

Even as conceived, there were major drawbacks to both designs. The Vanden Plas would have had to soldier on with the old chassis design and running gear – whose roots were in the 1940s – while Sir William Lyons was most reluctant to keep the virtu-

ally tool-room-constructed Daimler 4½-litre V8 engine in production. There were further complications since BMH wanted to keep the Vanden Plas factory in Kingsbury busy, whereas Lyons wanted to close down the slow-moving car assembly lines at Radford (preferring to turn Radford into a major engine, transmission and suspension manufacturing plant instead, as a 'feeder' to Browns Lane).

Industrial logic triumphed in a most intriguing and pragmatic way. Both the old limousines would be allowed to die at the same time, but only one new limousine would take their place. The new model would basically be a Jaguar, but would carry forward Daimler's heritage and would be assembled at the Vanden Plas factory in North London. BMH (later to become part of British Leyland) always liked to keep everyone happy by compromise and this seemed to be an excellent way of achieving accord.

The new project was given the code DS-420, which followed neatly on from DR450 for the displaced Daimler. The first post-war Daimler had been a DB and that sequence had been retained during the next twenty years. Styling, influenced not only by Sir William Lyons, but with input from Hooper's long-established traditions on earlier big

Daimlers, was settled around a massive 141in (3,581mm) wheelbase.

That much was easy to understand, but to replace both the obsolete types, which had employed massive box-section separate frames, the new car would effectively be a unit-construction car. Instead of a separate frame there would be the lower elements of a unit-construction shell – what is called the 'platform' in modern motor-industry-speak – based very closely on that of the ageing 420G, but lengthened and with the new limousine superstructure style welded to it.

Owing to the new DS420 having such a long wheelbase – 21in (533mm) longer than that of the Jaguar saloon – it meant that quite a lot of extra surgery was required to that platform, but all the essentials of the 420G, including the front and rear wheel track dimensions and all the running gear were retained unchanged.

One might ask why the limousine was not based on the platform of the up-and-coming, and still secret, XJ6 model. One reason, I am sure, is that project work on the DS420 began well before the XJ6 was finalized, and the other is that the 420G's platform was that important bit wider, heavier and more capable of being adapted to the larger Daimler structure.

It is also known that the Mk X/420G, which had been the most rigid developed by Jaguar up to that time, relied very little on its upper structure for its strength, so its platform would be an ideal base for modification in this way. This, of course, allowed Jaguar-Daimler to offer partly-completed cars as 'stand-alone' chassis for completion as hearses by specialist coachbuilders – a tiny, but important, market.

As a production car, the new DS420 was therefore really born at Pressed Steel, which built up a 420G platform chassis, complete with front bulkhead, inner wheel arches and some inner panels. This was then shipped to the Motor Panels Ltd factory in Foleshill,

Coventry, whose first task was to slice the floorpan, to insert a 21in (53cm) long additional section behind the location of the front seat, add suitable stiffening and weld up the whole. There was a new top-hat transverse section across the floor, along with two extra 4×3in (10×7.5cm) longitudinal box sections to maintain the beam strength.

Motor Panels Ltd, whose factory was close to the one-time Jaguar plant in Foleshill, had long been linked to Jaguar, through providing panels for cars like the D-Type and E-type models. Since it had also done much truck cab business with Leyland Motors (later British Leyland), it was well used to producing limited numbers of structures.

Having lengthened the platform, Motor Panels' next task was to shape all the special sheet metal panels unique to the new Daimler on simple tooling, then to assemble entire 'body-in-white' limousine shells. Given the numbers to be made – sales of more than 500 limousines a year could never have been forecast – the cars would have to be built on the simplest possible tooling, almost, in motor industry parlance, by 'knife-and-fork' methods.

Complete unpainted shells were then delivered to Kingsbury, close to the A5 Edgware Road in north-west London, where the shells were painted, trimmed, and completed, with all mechanical elements being supplied by Jaguar. Badged as Daimler Limousines, though acknowledged to have a great Vanden Plas content, these cars were really Jaguars built 'by remote control'.

Mechanically, the original Daimler Limousine was very similar to the 420G, though there were important differences. For this car the famous XK engine was in 420/Sovereign (not 420G) tune, which is to say that it used two 2in (50mm) SU carburettors and produced 245bhp (gross); this was matched to the latest Model 8 Borg Warner automatic transmission on all cars,

The Jaguar-designed Daimler Limousine, which sold slowly but regularly for more than twenty years, was built up on the basis of a lengthened Mk X/420G platform. Bodyshell construction was by Motor Panels of Coventry, and until 1979 final assembly was always carried out by Vanden Plas in Kingsbury, North London.

it being thought that manual transmission was simply not appropriate to a limousine of this type.

Although the suspension looked identical to that of the 420G, there were significant changes. To match the ride to the image of the Limousine, and because the new car weighed 700lb (317kg) more than the 420G, front spring rates were increased from 100 to 130lb/in (18 to 23kg/cm), while rear rates were increased from 150 to 178lb/in (27 to 32 kg/cm). Wheels and tyres, too, were larger than on the 420G. The ride of this new Daimler was developed with low speed comfort in mind, rather than high-speed handling, and the independent rear suspension must have helped a lot in this aim. Although it was never mentioned in any Daimler advertizing, salesmen always reminded their contacts, discreetly, that the competing Rolls-Royce Phantom V Limousine not only had a rigid rear axle, but drum brakes too.

In its body style, equipment and implied character, the new Limousine was almost totally different from the 420G, for it was lofty where the 420G was low, angular where the 420G was curvaceous, and spacious where the 420G was no more than conventionally roomy. Interestingly, the driving compartment of the Daimler was much less comfortable than that of the 420G, for there was no adjustment to the driver's seat. As happened so often with limousines, the designers could only provide a rather cramped seat with a fixed back-rest, which was fixed to the immovable vertical division itself.

Apart from the Limousine's great weight and bulk, just quoted above, a few other basic statistics tell their own story. Owing to its very long wheelbase, the new Daimler was no less than 23.5in (597mm) longer than the 420G. It was also 2.2in (56mm) wider, and (to provide 'top-hat headroom' through the passenger doors) it was a whopping 9.3in (236mm) higher.

By almost any standard, there was a colossal amount of space in the rear compartment. 'Walk-in' headroom was 47in (119cm), the distance across the car between side trim panels was 62.5in (159cm), and with the occasional seats folded down there was well over 36in (91cm) between the front of the rear seat and the division itself.

The Daimler also had a more ponderous turning circle – no less than 46ft (14m) – but this rarely mattered to the chauffeur, as his arrival was usually signalled well in advance, and space cleared accordingly!

Inside the cabin, particularly in the spacious rear area, there seemed to be acres of real leather, thick carpeting and wooden veneer, while there were two fold-up occasional seats (which could seat three abreast at a squeeze) ahead of the main rear seats. The list of optional extras was extensive (and expensive) for, apart from the usual items such as an electrically operated glass partition between front and rear seats, cocktail cabinets and separate rear-mounted radio sets, customers could also have darkened glass, TV receivers, two-way telephone contact between chauffeur and passengers, armour plating and bullet-proof glass, and any number of permutations on the seating shape and location.

The initial choice of body colour and trim materials was as discreet as you might expect. Black or Carlton Grey were standard, though Maroon, Dark Green, Light Grey or Dark Blue were also optional. Other colours could also be provided by special negotiation. Upholstery was either leather or West-of-England cloth.

Announced in June 1968, the new Limousine was originally built at Kingsbury at a rate of up to ten cars a week and, although this rate fell away in the 1970s to three or four a week, there was rarely a lack of orders to keep the Limousine team occupied. In 1968 the Limousine sold for £4,424 (before all those optional extra costs began to mount up), compared with £2,408 for a 420G saloon and £11,119 for a Rolls-Royce Phantom V Limousine.

Over the years, except for development changes shared with the 420G (and later with the XJ6 models), few innovations were ever applied to the mechanical equipment, and there was little retouching to the styling. Although it is really quite difficult to tell the difference between, say, a 1968 Limousine and one produced in the late 1980s, Daimler followers can point to a few recognition points.

From 1972 there were changes to the division, providing more glass and less framework, while the rear quarter windows became one piece and could be swivelled

rather than wound down. By 1980 the front style had been retouched, with smaller over-riders, rectangular flashing indicators, and re-shaped air intakes.

Two special landaulettes (with a fold-back soft-top over the rear seats) were built at Kingsbury in the 1970s, but all other versions were either Limousines or partly completed 'rolling chassis' supplied to coach-builders for completion as hearses.

British Leyland closed down the Vanden Plas Kingsbury factory in November 1979, choosing to transfer Limousine assembly to a special workshop at Jaguar's Browns Lane factory in Allesley. There was no question of setting up an actual assembly line for the Limousine was now an ideal candidate for

From 1979 Daimler Limousine assembly was moved back from Kingsbury to a dedicated corner of Jaguar's Browns Lane factory. This study of three bodyshells, freshly delivered from Motor Panels on the other side of Coventry, clearly show the Mk X/420G underpinnings, notably that characteristic 'chassis' strut from the front suspension cross-member region to the bulkhead.

Daimler Limousine assembly was always a slow, careful, hand-building process. Here, at Browns Lane, the final trimming is being applied to one of the cars, with two more partly-built machines in the background.

group assembly, with the cars stationary in their own dedicated corner. In many ways this was more convenient for the production planners, as the bodyshells only had to be transported a few miles across Coventry, from Motor Panels, while the engines made a similarly short journey from Radford.

Although 2,525 DS420 Limousines had been assembled at Kingsbury, the build rate at Allesley slowed down further. It was not that there was anything lacking in the Limousine's appeal, merely that the car's natural market was contracting all the time and the existing stock of Limousines was proving to be very long lived indeed.

By the mid-1980s fuel injection was available and many other improvements had been made to align the Limousine's 'chassis' more closely to that of the XJ6. From the

autumn of 1986, when Limousine prices began at £31,950, Jaguar announced that the Limousine would only be available to special order, but demand remained steady for some years after that. Further detail style changes in the autumn of 1987 included the use of deformable plastic bumpers, allied to a modified radiator grille.

Sales and assembly finally fell away in the early 1990s – 165 cars being built in 1990, 126 in 1991, but a mere 36 in 1992. The last Limousine of all was completed in October 1992, and left the factory for its customer in January 1993. A total of 4,206 of these noble machines had been produced in twenty-four years. With it went the last trace of Mk X/420G heritage from the Jaguar factory, although parts were still made available for most models.

Appendix B
Performance Summary

To repeat the old clichés – how could Jaguar do it at the price? Not only were the cars beautiful and fast, but they were also remarkable value for money.

Although I can't quantify elegance and value, there is a lot to be learned by looking at performance figures. With the blessing of *Autocar* and *Motor*, I have summarized *The Autocar* (later *Autocar*) road test figures quoted over the years:

Model	3½-Litre	Mk V (3.5-litre)	Mk VII (Overdrive)	Mk VIIM (Auto)
Engine power (gross bhp)	125	120	160	190
Mean maximum speed (mph)				
Overdrive top	–	–	N.Q.	–
Direct top	91	91	102	100
Third	67	65	70	–
Second/inter	46	46	46	68
First/low	27	27	28	39
Acceleration (sec)				
0–30mph	5.3	6.3	4.4	4.8
0–60mph	16.8	18.9	13.6	14.3
0–80mph	N.Q.	40.7	25.7	26.8
0–100mph	–	–	–	–
Standing ¼-mile (sec)	N.Q.	N.Q.	19.3	19.7
Overall fuel consumption (mpg)	16–18	15–18	20	18.5
Kerb weight (lb (kg))	3,640 (1,651)	3,717 (1,686)	3,864 (1,753)	3,941 (1,788)
Test published	March 1948	July 1949	Sept 1954	May 1956

[N.Q. = Not quoted]

Appendix B: Performance Summary

Model	Mk VIII (Auto)	Mk IX (Auto)	Mk X (3.8-litre) (Auto)	Mk X (4.2litre) (Auto)
Engine power (gross bhp)	210	220	265	265
Mean maximum speeds (mph)				
Overdrive top	–	–	–	–
Direct top	106.5	113.5	119.5	121.5
Third	–	–	–	–
Second/inter	72	80	82	76
First/low	46	48	51	47
Acceleration (sec)				
0–30mph	4.4	4.0	4.9	4.0
0–60mph	11.6	11.0	12.1	9.9
0–80mph	20.2	18.6	20.6	17.0
0–100mph	35.7	32.5	33.3	27.4
Standing ¼- mile (sec)	18.4	17.8	18.5	17.0
Overall fuel consumption (mpg)	17.9	14.4	14.1	14.5
Kerb weight (lb (kg))	4,040 (1,833)	3,997 (1,813)	4,179 (1,896)	4,151 (1,883)
Test published	Jan 1957	Dec 1958	Nov 1962	Oct 1964

Index